Britain's Educational Reform

THE NISSAN INSTITUTE/ ROUTLEDGE JAPANESE STUDIES SERIES

Britain's Educational Reform

A Comparison with Japan

Mike Howarth

London and New York

First published 1991
by Routledge
11 New Fetter Lane, London EC4P 4EE
Simultaneously published in the USA and Canada
by Routledge
a division of Routledge, Chapman and Hall, Inc.
29 West 35th Street, New York, NY 10001

© 1991 Mike Howarth

Typeset by Pat and Anne Murphy,
Highcliffe-on-Sea, Dorset.
Printed in Great Britain by
Billing & Sons Ltd, Worcester

British Library Cataloguing in Publication Data

Howarth, Mike, *1942–*
    Britain's educational reform: a comparison with Japan. –
    (Nissan Institute/Routledge Japanese studies series).
    1. Great Britain. Education. Reform.   2. Japan. Education.
    I. Title
    370′.941
    ISBN 0-415-03850-2

Library of Congress Cataloging in Publication Data

Howarth, Mike, 1942–
    Britain's educational reform: a comparison with Japan / Mike
Howarth.
        p.   cm. – (The Nissan Institute/Routledge Japanese studies
series)
    Includes bibliographical references.
    1. Education – Great Britain.   2. Education – Japan.
3. Educational innovations – Great Britain – Evaluation.
4. Comparative education.   I. Title.   II. Series.
LA632.H59   1990
370′.952–dc20
                                                                89-71067
                                                                CIP

For Cathy and Peter

Contents

Figures and tables

General editor's preface

Almost imperceptibly, during the 1980s, Japan has become 'hot news'. The successes of the Japanese economy and the resourcefulness of her people have long been appreciated abroad. What is new is an awareness of her increasing impact on the outside world. This tends to produce painful adjustment and uncomfortable reactions. It also often leads to stereotypes and arguments based on outdated or ill-informed ideas.

The Nissan Institute/Routledge Japanese Studies Series seeks to foster an informed and balanced – but not uncritical – understanding of Japan. One aim of the series is to show the depth and variety of Japanese institutions, practices, and ideas. Another is, by using comparison, to see what lessons, positive and negative, can be drawn for other countries. There are many aspects of Japan which are little known outside that country but which deserve to be better understood.

The present book represents a new departure for the series in two senses. First of all, it is primarily a critique of the current education system and education policy in England and Wales. The record of Japanese education in producing numerate and literate pupils not only among the highly intelligent but also among those of only average ability, is carefully explored and shown to have direct relevance to the educational problems of this country. Second, the author is himself the headteacher of a large comprehensive school in South Wales, who has much direct experience, at the 'chalk face', of the problems he analyses in this book. He himself knows Japanese and has introduced the study of Japan into his school. The combination of his expertise in Japanese education with his position as a headteacher within the maintained system of British education, gives a unique quality to this book.

Mike Howarth employs a deeply thoughtful approach, in which he seeks to adapt aspects of the Japanese education system to British conditions. He is not uncritical of the Japanese system but recognizes its strengths and the relevance of those strengths to Britain: namely that a serious attempt is made to educate the whole population, not just an elite; that structural incentives for pupils to progress exist throughout the system;

that there is a clear priority about what is to be taught and policy on curriculum is stable and comprehensible; that nearly everybody remains in school to age 18 and a high proportion enter a form of tertiary education; that education to age 18 is general rather than vocational; and that employers are able to give specific vocational training to young men and women whose level of general education can be taken more or less for granted.

I believe that this book is a pioneering exercise in exploring the relevance of Japanese experience in the improvement of British institutions and practices.

J. A. A. Stockwin
Director of the Nissan Institute of Japanese Studies,
University of Oxford

Acknowledgements

I am greatly indebted to Professor Arthur Stockwin, of the Nissan Institute for Japanese Studies, Oxford, not only for his expert opinion but also for the friendship and support without which this book could not have been written.

I wish to thank my colleagues in Mid-Glamorgan Education Authority who have always been ready to exchange views with me. This has been a great help in testing my own opinion. Particular thanks to my own staff for sharing their problems and views and forcing me constantly to think out my own position on issues raised in the book.

Irene Hughes, Mike Doyle and Dic Felstead read the first rough of the book and their comments were invaluable at subsequent stages. They also gave me the heart to take the work to completion. Merlith Thomas provided many of the industrial references.

The following members of the Japanese teaching profession gave unstintingly of their time and provided me with much material. Mr Miyata Takao, Headteacher, Maebashi Nishi Kotogakko, Gunma-ken and members of his staff, particularly Mr Morita Makoto and Mr Suzuki Chiharu, made me very welcome in their school and admitted me to their meetings. I am grateful for the continued link between my school and theirs and to the English language assistants Suzanne Parkhurst and Kathy Oswin who have helped to sustain it. Mr Yamanaka Chikara, Headteacher, Misato Kita Chugakko, Saitama-ken and his staff were of inestimable value in giving me first hand experience of the Japanese education system. My thanks to the heads of the other junior high schools of Misato-City for their time given to exchanging views with me. The members of the first young teachers' study tour to Britain, Mr Matsunami Yasushi, Mr Ishihara Kazuko, Mr Yamada Michio, Mr Enjoji Takeshi and Mr Sukekawa Koki spent an exhausting time in my school answering questions as well as asking them. Mr Sukekawa, especially, I must thank for his friendship and the arrangements made for my visit to Misato Kita.

The leading executives of Japanese companies in Wales have been most helpful. My special thanks to Mr Murayama of

Matsushita Electric UK, Mr Nakano of Aiwa UK, Mr Tokita and Mr Nakamura of Sony UK.

To Miss Matsui Midori, the lady who made my interest in Japan a reality by teaching me the language and introducing me to the community, I must express my eternal gratitude. Three other ladies, Mrs Murayama Sumiko, Mrs Okamoto Kyoko and Mrs Nakanishi Shuko were also highly instrumental in giving me whatever language proficiency I have. The Yoshida, Akiyama, Tosaki, Abe, Sukekawa and Ito families have given me limitless hospitality on my visits to Japan.

My wife, Shirley, provided a constant test of opinion and was rewarded with the thankless task of proof reading the final typescript.

1

Background to change

The tides of change in British education will, for better or worse, transform the system. They threaten, at the chalk face, to drown it in confusion. This book attempts to assess the changes from another perspective – that of Japan – in the hope that a more distant view will help clarify our objectives and intentions.

Some of the recent initiatives in British educational change, like the national curriculum, are tried and tested in many parts of the world, even if its content, the limited compass of its age range and assessment methods are not. Others, like the Technical and Vocational Education Initiative (TVEI) and its extension TVE, presently being implemented nationwide, are new inventions. So too are the changes in the governance and financing of schools. The *combination* of change is unique; its scale unprecedented. It is characteristically British in its idiosyncrasy.

No less striking are the attempts to change national attitudes towards training for employment. A significant reappraisal of our needs, and of the institutions to deliver training, seems to be taking hold of the national imagination. A parallel development, giving hope for the future, is the preparedness of some industries to take a fresh look at themselves. An advancing mood of company entrepreneurship seems to be matched in some of the unions, like the engineers and electricians, with the willingness to consider new forms of industrial relations – the growth of single-union representation is an encouraging example of new attitudes.

Change has not been uniformly welcomed. Large segments of the education system have opposed it inch by inch. Many teachers wish to stick to ways that have served them – but not all their pupils – well in the past. Some of the vested interests in higher education will be amongst the slowest to yield their protected ground. Many companies remain unenlightened about the need for training as do many potential trainees. Perhaps a majority of unions, though not necessarily their grass-root members, oppose the erosion, as they see it, of their traditional powers.

Most of the changes presently under way have yet to show their full effects; many have barely begun to scratch the surface of problems they were designed to meet. However, we are still at the stage where modifications can be made as we go along, where some reappraisal of the likely outcome of initiatives can be made and where factors not yet really considered can find an input.

More importantly we need to ask whether the changes are the right ones. Are they aimed in the right direction and sufficient; or are they misdirected or superfluous? It is my intention to examine these changes from the main perspective available to me – from within the British education system. It is at the chalk face that the rhetoric of change will be translated into activity; where the impact of change will be most keenly felt and where successes and failures will first manifest themselves.

In an attempt to assess the likely impact of change in education and training I have used Japan as a comparator. It is a country I have studied for the last decade and a half and the only one, outside my own, whose language I understand passably well. In some parts of this book, Britain may appear to compare very unfavourably with Japan. This is partly because of the near impossibility of comparing like with like. Also, I have elected deliberately, in many cases, to compare the best in Japan with the worst in Britain without redressing the balance. The intention of this 'unfair' approach is only to point out better ways in which we might tackle our problems.

'Unfair' it may be, but my approach is not entirely invalid. The worst in Britain has had, I believe, a more powerful effect on our society, in the post-war years, than the best. The opposite, I think is true of Japan; the best, on the whole, has outweighed the worst. This is not to say Japan is without very serious faults; that would be too much to expect of any large developed nation. I have, however, only given these as much space as is needed to balance the picture where they are relevant to the theme. The larger problems of Japan, outside the scope of this book, I have been content to leave to Japanese writers. These are more their concern than mine.

Where Japanese methods, ways of looking at problems or the solutions attempted do not seem reproducible in Britain, I have tried to avoid them whatever their merits might be in Japan. Features that depend entirely on cultural differences, for instance, are unlikely to be useful imports. My intention is to suggest what might be helpful to Britain – not to admire Japan. Some Japanese methods contain useful elements alongside others that should be avoided. In these cases I have tried to dissect the good from the bad. In other areas, Japanese methods would require adaptation before they could be applied to Britain. There are very few cases where outright imitation of Japanese methods would be appropriate. Britain and Japan are very different countries. We need to look at Japanese ways of doing things and scrutinize them for their potential adaptability to British needs. In some cases it will be sufficient if we recognize that there are other ways of doing things, of looking at a problem, and rethink some of our own methods and assumptions. This has been the Japanese way in cases where they have borrowed from the West, Professor J.A.A. Stockwin in a commentary on Ezra Vogel's *Japan As Number One* (1979) wrote:

> It is questionable how far it is possible to transplant the institutions and practices of one culture . . . into another, although it is as well to remember that the strangeness may stem from the fact that the proposed transplantation is from East to West. It has often in the past seemed less surprising when the influence was in the opposite direction.
>
> (private communication to author 1987)

Many factors have conspired in Britain's economic failure. It will be worth a very brief summary of the important ones recognizing that improvement in education and training alone will not solve our problems.

SOME FACTORS IN BRITAIN'S POOR ECONOMIC PERFORMANCE

1 State structures
2 Industrial and company structure
3 Financial markets
4 Party politics

5 Industrial relations
6 Attitudes of the people – especially class
7 Misdirection and incoherence in education and training

It is obviously beyond the scope of this book to tackle all of these in other than the sketchiest outline. I have devoted one chapter to each of items 2 and 6 and within those have made passing reference to the other items. All the rest of the book is given to item 7. For the purposes of introduction, however, a very brief review of all these items follows here to give perspective to the rest of the book.

1 STATE STRUCTURES

In *Start Again Britain*, Sir Charles Villiers, former head of British Steel, proposed the idea of a 'development state' which he defined as:

> The main purpose of the development state in Britain would be the long-term improvement of Britain's real economy, and all that bears upon it. It would develop all Britain's assets: men, women, skills, experience, machines, bricks, mortar, minerals and, of course, financial assets. This would be done by voluntary collaboration between government, management, schools, colleges, customers and workforce, leaving companies completely free in the market places. This purpose would take priority over everything except national defence, dignity and liberty – and you don't get much of them if you can't afford to pay!

(Villiers 1984)

This is not mere pious exhortation. The remarkable thing about Sir Charles's book is that he goes on to give practical ways in which the development state could be brought about. He regards it as a successor to the welfare state and one in which the 'needy' are better cared for. He sees great similarities between the development state and the post-war Japanese state and quotes Professor Chalmers Johnson of the University of California: 'Throughout the fifties the Japanese government operated and perfected what is recognised today as a model of the state-guided capitalist development system.' A similar and more frequently quoted comment that the Japanese economy is 'the most intelligently dirigiste system in the world today'. (*Economist* May 1967) also points to the strengths of the Japanese state structure in promoting economic success.

These views hardly apply today and Japan may never have been as straightforwardly 'state guided' as the comments insist. Comparisons between Japan and a joint stock company – 'Japan Inc.' – (e.g. Abegglen 1971 and the much less balanced views in Wolf 1983) are overplayed. Japan's economic society has evolved over the years and the role of planning agencies like the Ministry of International Trade and Industry, MITI, now play a rather different role. A much fairer assessment of the role of government in the Japanese economy is given in Stockwin (1975: Chapter 8).

The Japanese government did give a strong indicational lead in the post-war economic recovery. The extent to which it is able to promote coherence across the economic spectrum, including education and training, is in my view still considerably greater than is the case in Britain. Our primary economic policy-making organ, the Treasury, has shown little familiarity with, or concern for, the progress of industry (Hall 1986). In Chapter 7, I have looked a little more closely at the inappropriateness of background, outlook, and education of our civil service elite. In a comparison of eight major industrialized countries Britain ranked last in its capacity to implement manpower policy (Wilensky and Turner 1987). Indeed, it was not until the 1973 creation of the MSC that the state had an organ for active labour market policy. A shortage of labour market statistics made manpower projections of future skill requirements a near impossibility (Reid 1980). No doubt 'state-guided capitalism' is further than Mrs Thatcher's government would be prepared, or should want, to go. Nevertheless, in the reform of education law and in the national training initiatives the government is taking a whole-nation lead as policy maker and ethos setter. I, for one, welcome this even though for much of this book I shall be giving less than wholehearted support to some of the government's measures.

In the 1950s, following a war in which she lost millions of lives, 40 per cent of her capital stock, her reputation and her illusions, Japan was in a 'start again' situation. It might be useful to think of ourselves as being in a similar condition in the late 1980s. If we do not; if we think the fault lies elsewhere and that we, *as the state*, have nothing to contribute; if we insist on our rights before our responsibilities; if we prefer antagonism to co-operation and tolerate incompetence rather than seeking improvement, then we shall fail to emerge from the economic crisis we have begun to tackle.

We have much to learn from, and much in common with Japan. It would be foolish to ignore the lessons Japan learned, and the systems she developed, as she trod the road towards the 'development state' ahead of us.

2 INDUSTRIAL AND COMPANY STRUCTURE

For many years I have watched Japan succeed in enterprises that are reproducible in Britain but in which we have failed. The Japanese have shown confidence in areas where our nerve appears to have deserted us. Why is Nissan, for example, sure that it can make a car manufacturing operation succeed in the north east of England? Almost any advanced nation can design a good car; car-making is not the most high-tech industry in the modern world. It is one, however, out of many examples, that is highly responsive to good company practice and organization. Why should Japanese managers make a better job of managing British workers than our own managers? In fact Nissan has paid us a great compliment. It is, in effect, acknowledging that we have a workforce that can be trained in new techniques and attitudes to work. Nissan takes great pride in its Geordies even if, seemingly, Britain does not. What is wrong with the way we are doing things?

Only a small minority of British companies has experimented with advanced manufacturing technologies. Management plans are still predominantly directed towards traditional mass-production market segments (New and Meyers 1986). Britain is still heavily dependent upon low-skill, continuous-process manufacture. In comparison, companies like Nissan and Toyota, in their Japanese plants, use the 'just-in-time' (JIT) system to 'pull' parts through the manufacturing system eliminating the need to hold stocks and the storage of work in progress. High vertical integration with their suppliers ensures deliveries of exactly the quantities of parts needed several times a day. The highly trained workforce, in Japan, is capable of shifting from one short-run batch to another without loss of 'down time' in re-tooling. So effective is the Nissan system in

Japan, through computer connection to the retail outlets, that each car, in the combinations of model, colour, engine capacity, seat and upholstery and all the other variables of an individual customer's choice, has passed through the assembly system within about 4 hours designated to that particular customer. Nissan has been able to reduce batch production down to the ideal of 'the single unit' – individual customization at the mass-production level (see Chapter 8).

British firms, where they have introduced new technologies, have tended to use these to de-skill work (Streeck 1985) instead of using the technology to increase flexibility and expand job definitions (Scarborough 1986). This has been particularly true in the automation of car production, a marked deficiency in comparison with Japan.

Studies of 2,500 British firms showed that more than half made no provision for management training (Anderson 1987). The low emphasis on management training and the low regard accorded to technical higher education and management schools result from the accountancy mindedness of British industry. It is highly unlikely, if it sees no need for its own training, that British management will place a high priority on it for other employees. Training is much more likely to be viewed as an overhead than an investment.

3 FINANCIAL MARKETS

Britain suffers from the inadequate financing of industry. There is an historical separation between financial and industrial capital with a concentration on the former (Pollard 1981; Hall 1986; Mayer 1987). Easy access to capital has assisted the growth of Japanese industry (Hedberg 1972; Carrington and Edwards 1981). British and American financial institutions have proved very inadequate in this respect. Expansion has had to occur in industry out of retained profits. This has resulted in accountancy rather than production as the major element in the industrial 'short termism' of British management thinking. The poor financing of British industry is aggravated by the need for companies to consume much of their profits by giving dividends to shareholders in order to maintain the company share value on the stock exchange. Japanese industry is much freer from this need and much higher levels of profit can be retained for investment. Companies give only notional dividends that do not reflect true profitability. The market esteem accorded to a company is not affected to the same degree by declared dividends. Ironically the Japanese shareholder has benefited from this type of arrangement – the shares have risen rapidly in value and returned a good profit when subsequently sold. The comparative balance of advantage is towards the Japanese, rather than British or American shareholder (Abegglen and Stalk 1985).

4 PARTY POLITICS

I have given space in Chapter 7 to the attitudes that engender, sustain and result from party politics. For the purposes of setting national goals Britain has been unfortunate in having parties with quite different priorities alternating in government. At least one of these, the Labour Party, has always maintained a strong ideological base and party dogma has often been viewed as of more importance than practical measures. Since the early 1980s there has been developed, in the Conservative Party, an opposite and equally powerful dogma, the belief that privatization and competition will, by freeing market forces, bring about appropriate change. It is hard to see how this view would, for example, produce rational plans for a transport network connected with the Channel tunnel competitive with developments in continental Europe where government agencies have been very actively involved. Our side of the development is a penny-packet mess of uncoordinated initiatives. The same unfavourable comparisons can be made of our port structure compared with the development of Rotterdam, Antwerp, and the French ports. The competing party stances on the institutions intended to give frame to the operation of industry can be inferred from Table 1.1.

5 INDUSTRIAL RELATIONS

The authority structure of British companies and the existence of unions that run across different companies, and even different sectors of industry, have combined to produce an antagonistic rather than co-operative view of industrial relations. Both the CBI and the TUC lack the power, at the level of individual

Table 1.1 Fluctuation government economic bodies, 1962–79

Institution	Date set up	By whom	Date abolished	By whom
Nat Incomes Commission	1962	Con	1964	Lab
Prices and Incomes Board	1964	Lab	1970	Con
Industrial Reorganization Corp	1966	Lab	1970	Con
Comm for Industrial Relations	1969	Lab	1970	Con
Pay Board	1970	Con	1974	Lab
Nat Indust Relations Court	1971	Con	1974	Lab
Min Trade and Consumer Affairs	1972	Con	—	—
Expansion of MTCA (above)	1974	Lab	1979	Con
Price Commission	1973	Con	—	—
Expansion of Price Commission	1974	Lab	1979	Con
Nat Enterprise Board	1975	Lab	1979*	Con

Source: Constructed from text of Owen (1986)
* Restructured.

companies, to exert any real co-ordinating influence. The British have the most complex trade-union system in the world (Clegg 1972). The TUC has immense difficulties in dealing with the system to provide desirable objectives like training. The response of the CBI to similar objectives is to adopt a non-interventionist approach and to claim that market forces will prompt whatever action is needed (Keep 1986). It is fair to ask whether this is a valid policy approach or simply throwing in the towel and making a virtue out of necessity by claiming that non-action is the solution to the problem. The result of such a policy, as distinct from the philosophy behind it, is gross under-training.

6 ATTITUDES OF THE PEOPLE

Historically, Britain is a class-ridden country and shows little inclination to remove social barriers in the present day. In 1975 the former West German Chancellor Helmut Schmidt said to Harold Wilson, 'as long as you maintain that damned class-ridden society of yours, you will never get out of your mess' (Villiers 1984). We are greatly divided in wealth and in the rewards we give for different tasks. We are divided between north and south; between decline and relative prosperity. A left–right split divides us politically and is unable to reach much consensus about economic and social objectives.

The Hudson Report – *The United Kingdom to 1980* – suggested that specific remedies for Britain's ills would be ineffective without a change in style, without a deep shift in psychology, a change of will.

> Britain's present economic . . . and social difficulties derive ultimately from a kind of archaism of the society and national psychology: a habit of conciliation in social and personal relations for its own sake, a lack of aggression, a deference to what exists, a repeated and characteristic flight into pre-industrial, indeed pre-capitalist fantasies, a suspicion of efficiency as somehow common, a dislike for labour itself – all, of course, accompanied by a deep inner rage at the frustrations and obfuscations which contemporary Britain demands of its citizens and an equally significant envy for the worldly goods that others . . . have and which the stodgy pattern of a more traditionalist British society and economy cannot provide.
>
> (Coates and Hillard (eds) 1986)

That was how the writers of the Hudson report saw Britain in 1974. Sixteen years later, despite a largely wasted oil bonanza, the changes of government and the coming and going of economic creeds, there are signs, in education and training that the situation is beginning to alter. What we must avoid is the complacency that has nowhere been more apparent than in the British attitudinal capacity to jump over the present and immediate, urgent future to a distant, unreal, and brighter tomorrow in which the problems do not require confrontation – a kind of romantic time-warp. Unfortunately there are signs, in the recent educational change, that this attitudinal dysfunction is not entirely absent. The government's belief that 'competition' in education will lead to a desirable state in some unspecified future, for example, ignores urgent problems in the schools today. What will the legislation do about truancy, disruption of classrooms, our staying-on rate and the muddle of post-16 education?

Britain is particularly prone to idiosyncratic solutions: '[I was] . . . increasingly impatient of Britain's addiction to believing it always knew best even though its recipes ended only too frequently in doing worst' (Roy Jenkins 1989).

We might have spared a thought that the uniqueness of

Britain's educational reforms might itself be a warning light to us. Perhaps a little more prudence, a look at what others were doing, would not have come amiss.

INCOHERENCE AND MIS-DIRECTION IN EDUCATION AND TRAINING

Readers will forgive a headmaster his prejudices, but it is my belief that most of the problems that beset Britain, have their source in the divisiveness that is both a characteristic and an effect of our education system. *The Independent* newspaper of 15 January 1987 carried a startling cartoon by Daley. The education systems of Britain, France, Germany and Japan were represented as flowering shrubs. Those of Japan and Germany were conical and bushy with flowers right down to the base of the stem. France had a good top but only a few flowers on the stalk. Britain showed a stem on which the flowers had failed to develop. Only at the very top were blossoms to be found.

Britain created a school system geared to the few who are capable of going on to study advanced-level subjects in the sixth form or who would comprise our tiny higher education intake. Even amongst these, our academic best, a cultural divide is perpetuated by narrow over-specialization from a too early stage; our best educated are in danger of not communicating effectively even amongst themselves. There is very damaging under-education elsewhere. A large proportion of pupils leave school ill-equipped to deal with the modern world. Of pupils continuing education beyond compulsory age, Britain has one of the lowest proportions of any developed nation (Maclure, 1988a). Britain was the only country in the OECD to have a falling rate of staying-on for 16–19 education in the 1970s. In the 1980s our ranking in OECD remains unchanged. Although the rate has risen slightly it has not done so to a degree that will help us catch up with the other countries (OECD 1985).

In effect, Britain has evolved a 'push-through' system of education. The efforts in teaching and learning, in the compulsory period of education, squeeze a small proportion through a narrow bottleneck into post-compulsory and higher education. The rest, discouraged by the narrowness of the bottleneck, leave education. Indeed, their education may have been differentiated to such a degree at an early stage that their capacity to get

11

through the bottleneck is nil. British companies remain relatively ignorant about how to capitalize on the usefulness of education and hence offer few incentives and motivators to energize progression through the education system. I can understand the reasoning that prompts the remark 'Britain needs more students as urgently as it needs more shipbuilders' (Murphy: TES 20.1.89). It is made from a viewpoint that does not challenge the methods of British employers.

Japanese companies do utilize, to a much greater degree, the educational level of their employees. They offer high inducement to enter the companies, or to compete to enter through educational standard. Similarly the Japanese post-compulsory and higher education sectors have a much wider intake which is more highly motivating to the generality of students. The neck of the bottle is much wider. The compulsory sector educates all through a universal national curriculum with little or no differentiation. The Japanese system can, much more easily, be seen as a 'pull-through' system, energized from the employment end, and pulling (or motivating) large numbers to pass through from all levels of the education system.

In essence, the nature of the educational divide is that the British lack the common cultural capital, and the high standards of *general education*, that most of our competitors have. This segregates us internally and weakens us in the face of their progressive economies and more rapidly evolving societies. Our uncommonly low standards of general education restrict the possibilities that might be achieved by vocational education and training, VET, subsequent to schooling:

A . . . factor that constrains the UK's VET performance is the small size of the UK's post-compulsory education system relative to those possessed by nearly every other developed nation. The numbers remaining after 16 are lower in the UK than in the USA, Japan, or most European countries, and the proportion of the relevant age group in Britain going on to higher education is also much lower.

(Keep and Mayhew 1988)

It is a little beyond the scope of this book to examine the exact relationship between education training and economic progress of a nation. That a high correlation between these exists will be taken for granted under the general validity of human capital theory (Becker 1975). There are specific advantages from education even when the job target is unsepcific: 'the economic value of much, perhaps most, education is less direct [than a doctor's for example]. For education . . . increases the capacity to learn and thereby increases the cost-effectiveness of later training' (White 1988).

What is beyond all doubt is that, in the advanced nations, there has been a marked shift in employment from low-skill to high-skill and low-knowledge occupations to high ones. Whilst the industries that employed people in essentially labouring or single-craft functions have matured and show slow growth or have actually declined, those employing high technical skills or using knowledge have increased. The outstanding examples are in information technology and its applications (Goldthorpe 1980; Goldthorpe and Payne 1986; Whitley, Wilson, and Smith 1980).

More pertinently to the major themes of this book, *at all levels of employment* there is a pressing economic need to improve educational standards and trainability. As a Japanese manager summed up the situation:

the intelligence of a handful of technocrats . . . is no longer enough. Only by drawing on the brainpower of all its employees can a firm face up to the turbulence and constraints of today's environment. This is why our large companies . . . demand from the education system increasing numbers of graduates as well as bright and well educated generalists.

(NEDC 1984)

The debate surrounding the contribution education should make towards economic progress is hindered by the existence of a dichotomy in the attitudes of educators. This dichotomy is perhaps best respresented by its poles. On the one hand is the 'education for its own sake' camp taking its thinking from the great nineteenth-century liberal tradition, resisting the incursion of trade and industry connections, denying that education should be connected to the vocational progression in any systematic form, eschewing the 'merely practical' and resistant to the changes proposed by the opposite pole of the dichotomy. The other camp seeks to bring 'relevance' into the curriculum and frequently interprets this as direct vocational input, seeks overt connections with the world of work and espouses a rhetoric similar to that used in 'training'.

Most educators in my experience lie, attitudinally, somewhere along the spectrum between these poles. The outcome of the dichotomy as it operates at the school level is early segregation of pupils *no matter which pole is dominant in a particular school.*

The 'education for its own sake' group finds the richest expression of its ideals in the brighter pupils and the A-level candidate where clear attainment of the ideology is demonstrable. Though the most humanitarian supporters of this camp would include the whole ability range within the compass of their ideals, their arguments are more difficult to support in the case of the less academic child who may incline to concrete rather than abstract operations. The view of this pole is likely, in many cases, to be challenged by parents who view education as providing a practical and specific toolbag for the future. In practice, the school is likely to adopt systems that segregate out its best potential success for a special treatment.

If the opposite pole is dominant, vocational connection is likely to begin at a quite early stage. The well-meaning efforts of the curriculum planners, in the school, result in early identification of pupils for whom differentiated educational diets will be appropriate and 'relevant'. The training ethos is presented to pupils of a tender age. Such might be the case where the Certificate of Education courses, pioneered by my own LEA and now available nationwide, form a dominant part of the curriculum of the less able. The prevalance of courses such as Vocational Studies, Leisure Studies, Traffic Education and Child Care within this provision for 14–16 year olds indicates a recognition, by the school, that some basic *and specific* skilling for work or after-school life is an objective of, or at least a vehicle for education.

An examination of the Japanese education system might indicate that the dichotomy need not exist, that it is, in fact, illusory. If I were slightly to overstate my case initially, I suppose I would say that the second pole has a correct motivation (work/life preparation – and unarguable intention) and the first pole is the more likely to achieve it (good education unencumbered by immediate considerations about the world of work). In other words, the best vocational preparation is good and prolonged general education not vocational education.

The failure of the 'education for its own sake' camp is that it has never really provided good *general education for all to a sufficiently high level and to a sufficiently advanced age.* It has been guilty of under-expectation by tacit recognition of a leaving age of 16-plus for all but the most able. It has thus conspired by default to project educationally unprepared youngsters into a work and life situation. The economic consequence has been the subsequent relative untrainability of these school leavers when compared with Japan.

The faults of the opposite camp are perhaps worse. Their actions have opportunity costs on general education by the imposition of early specifics of 'work and life' experiences into the curriculum, particularly of the lower half of the ability range. By the denial of good general education to a late age in favour of low-skill specifics, they have encouraged lack of adaptability in the school leavers. Their actions have produced a level of untrainability that only prolonged education could cure. For example, course elements in school, directed at preparing pupils for YTS, would strike me as the ultimate in low expectation. In educational terms they are worthless; in economic terms perversely intent on maintaining our low-skill equilibrium.

The good general education provided for almost all to the age of 18 in Japan, an education that does not concern itself too much with vocational specifics, has generated both a well educated population and a highly trainable workforce. Even those youngsters who opt for vocational upper secondary schools (about one-third of the 94 per cent staying on beyond compulsory schooling) spend the majority of their time in continuing general education (see Chapter 6).

Britain has been plagued not only by misdirection in education but by incoherence between the constituent parts of the system. We have piled muddle upon confusion and compromise on to fudge. We have consistently confused intentions and outcomes as if the latter were the last things that mattered.

It is possible to make severe criticisms of the Japanese education system. There is perhaps a too rigid emphasis, throughout the society, on educational qualifications, perhaps to the neglect of other attributes. The system imposes a very high pressure on students – this may even begin in kindergarten – and it is possible to construe the system as a type of 'force-feeding'. It is difficult to decide to what extent the relative high degree of uniformity in Japanese society is due to cultural attributes in general or the education system in particular. The Japanese style of teaching, which tends to be relatively didactic, finds little favour with British educationalists in particular, 'considerable emphasis [is] put on mathematics both in terms of time spent and the repetitious practice of basic skills. This has not been without cost' (National Curriculum Working Group for Mathematics: DES 1988).

The working group had other criticisms of the Japanese system arising from their study visit. Many of these seem to me quite valid when viewed in isolation. These, and others will be mentioned later in the book.

What is more difficult to challenge is the structural coherence of the Japanese system right the way through from primary school to employment in companies where high degrees of training are generally evident. There can be little doubt, either, that the system is not simply structured but structured for success. It is significant that, although the companies are the primary energizers of the 'pull-through' system of education, this has not produced vocationalism in Japanese schools.

Later sections of the book will examine Japan's national curriculum as it operates from primary to the end of upper-secondary school. We shall ask what, within this coherent system, has produced the world's highest staying-on rate beyond compulsory schooling. Extrinsic motivators appear to be built into the structure to ensure high general performance at all stages (Lynn 1988).

To a much greater degree than in Britain, we shall see that training is left to private companies but that good inducements to train are present. Training has the best of all possible starts – well educated people leaving the education sector. We shall see that Japan is not obsessed with the 'modularization' and 'skill-level' definition that plagues our attempts to construct better training systems but rather operates the 'driving-test' principle of relating performance to particular function (Dore and Sako: 1987 and 1988).

In comparison, it will be worthwhile highlighting Britain's lack of structural coherence in education – lack of clarity in aims and ambiguous or contradictory routes to solutions. These are deficiencies that have led to a great deal of under-performance at all levels of the education and vocational education and training (VET) systems.

Before any of the measures in the Education Reform Act (ERA) are examined in any detail, an assessment of the extent to which they might address the problem of incoherence should be briefly attempted. The exercise will serve, also, to introduce the range of measures to readers who are not already familiar with them. Issues concerned with training will be looked at in Chapter 8.

A SUMMARY OF THE CHANGES

The present round of educational reforms could be regarded as starting with the Ruskin College speech by James Callaghan in 1976. He raised questions about the effectiveness and accountability of education and opened the way for proper debate. In 1985 the DES issued *Better Schools* (Cmnd 9469), the seminal document that gave rise to the changes implemented in the 1988 Education Reform Act. A good practical guide to the implications of the Reform Act is contained in *Education Reformed* (Maclure 1988a).

One of the most important points to consider, in a summary of the changes currently underway, is whether a coherent package can be discerned. Do the changes hang together or do they contradict one another in ways that will mutually diminish their effectiveness? Because the government's economic objectives are influential motivators for change, it is important to decide what cultural overview, if any, can be deduced from a consideration of the whole set and whether this is consistent with the problem. In the terms of reference of this book, will they achieve the structural coherence that is an evident contributor to the success of the Japanese education system?

My general conclusions are that:

1 The set of changes seem to demonstrate a general philosophical belief, on the part of the government, that competition will lead to improvement. This is quite consistent with the general tenor of the government's view of almost every issue.

The Education Reform Bill permits 'opting out' of LEA control by individual schools into grant-maintained status which is effectively direct government funding. Establishments that do this are free from the damping constraint LEAs might apply on competition between schools. The power of LEAs is further diminished by the increased powers given to governing bodies of

17

schools. Furthermore, schools will be allowed open enrolment of pupils up to a high maximum and thus are further encouraged to compete for pupils. They will be in charge of their own budgets under the proposals for Local Management of Schools (LMS), yet another reduction in LEA power and a 'freeing-up' of competition. Funding of Higher Education will be made competitive. The former MSC was allowed to involve itself directly in education as the controlling agency of the Technical and Vocational Educational Initiative (TVEI) and its extension (TVE). Entry into the latter is through competitive bidding by LEAs. Some LEAs have determined the entry of schools into the local programme by competitive entry of TVE submissions.

2   There is nothing intrinsic, in the operation of market forces, that would lead to the development of a coherent package. In fact the opposite is more likely to apply when related to the reform of an already piecemeal system by the bolting-on of new structures especially where these are more doctrinaire than practical and are frequently contradictory.

New examinations like GCSE, that contain a high degree of organizational complexity like course work, differentiation of the examination level pupils will take according to ability and components of internal assessment, imply cross-school and whole LEA collaboration to make the best use of the talents residing in teaching staff. Competition between schools is irrelevant to such initiatives, or is actually damaging. The same applies to the delivery of the Extension of the Technical and Vocational Educational Initiative (TVE) where delivery of courses will most often need to be sought through collaborative consortia at the local level, exactly the point where competition is fiercest.

It would seem logical, however undesirable, for a government that was interested in pure competition between schools, as opposed to between pupils, to have avoided a national curriculum. A curicular free-for-all, where the education on offer was determined only by the market imperative of attracting as many pupils as possible, would seem to be the natural companion to the government's obsession to introduce competition. It would have the added advantage of giving parents the last say, as consumers, over what was taught, however bizarre this may have turned out to be in some cases.

There is a possible place, however, for a national curriculum in a more regulated competition strategy: 'Statutory control or standardisation of a service . . . helps the functioning of certain types of markets by reducing information costs to the users of the service' (White 1988). The parents are in a better position to judge the differences between schools' achievements if all the schools are attempting to achieve the same thing.

3 The set of measures is incoherent in several ways that are likely to reduce the overall effectiveness of the changes and in some cases reinforce existing confusions.

In particular, the progression routes for the majority beyond school remain muddled, contradictory and limited. The government acknowledges the need to increase the take-up of education beyond school-leaving age but has retained the YTS which gives 16-year olds a financial incentive to do the opposite. Staying on rates have actually declined since the introduction of two year YTS (DES 1987). Routes into 16-plus education have been complicated by the introduction of TVE criteria (see Chapter 6). Private schools are exempt from the national curriculum requirements. Will this leave them free to dominate the ranks of our ruling elites as they do at present? The opening of City Technology Colleges, CTCs, introduces a new type of school to complicate an already confusing array of provision. CTCs are intended to foster staying on until 18-plus (Taylor 1988). If they respond to the spirit of the Education Reform Bill 'to provide for pupils of different abilities' (ERB clause 80), by recruiting proportionately across the ability spectrum they may help to achieve this objective. If, on the other hand, they succumb to the temptation to recruit a disproportionate number from the higher-ability ranges, that is, pupils who are likely to stay on in any case, nothing will have been done for the overall national staying-on rate.

4 Measures vital to the attainment of real economic progress have been left out of the package.

One of Britain's major economic obstacles, a low general level of education in the majority of the population, because schooling for more than 50 per cent ends at 16-plus, remains untackled. The opportunity to increase staying-on rates, which if anything, have fallen in recent years, has not been thought fitting for the educational reforms. The chance to introduce a national curriculum to 18-plus was missed.

There is a perverse and determined failure in Britain to recognize that low-skill jobs are on the decline, or ought to be if we are to compete with countries like Japan, and that more highly skilled occupations should be on the increase. The government has perpetuated the mis-match between the economic objective and how we achieve it educationally. Or it has mis-perceived the economic objective.

Britain's current high growth rate, which exceeds that of most countries except Japan, may be short-term and illusory. The Conservatives have operated a number of supply-side measures that have increased efficiency of low-cost production and services. Thus the weakening of wage councils and employment security legislation, subsidising the creation of low-wage jobs and attacking unions have improved company profits (Finegold and Soskice 1988). Growth has been concentrated in the low-cost, low-skill production and service sectors. Current growth rates hide our failure to invest in a long-term high-skill future. YTS has helped employers to screen large numbers of low-skilled young workers and select the most socialized and willing (Chapman and Tooze 1987):

● The irony is that while Britain is striving to compete more effectively with low-cost producers such as South Korea and Singapore, these nations are investing heavily *in general education and training* to enable their industries to move into flexible, high technology production [my italics].

(Finegold and Soskice 1988)

These newly industrializing countries are, in other words following the route Japan established after the war. Britain remains 'trapped in a low skills equilibrium'.

The potential of GCSE and a national curriculum to produce improvement is diminished by an early cut-off point at 16-plus that releases an unacceptable proportion of leavers, having low-educational standards by international comparison, into dead-end futures that perpetuate our low-equilibrium economy. Thus we have a YTS scheme that cannot tackle, for most of them, much more than low-skill training. Between April 1986 and January 1988, 76.8 per cent of trainees left YTS without any qualifications (unpublished figures from MSC in White 1988). Many of the leavers enter low-skilled employment direct from school. The proportion taking this route may increase with the falling numbers of young people in the population and the consequent relative ease in finding a job (Jackson 1988). Thus even the limited potential of YTS to increase competence may be diminished.

5 Highly ambiguous processes have been instituted that confuse the direct work of teaching establishments. Many of them could have a subtractive effect on the time and money devoted to the main aims of education. Many could be characterized as needless complication.

Large amounts of time, energy and money have been spent on the government's attempts to involve parents in the running of schools. The annual general report now required for presentation at a meeting for parents costs in the region of £22,000 per annum, in a district of ten medium-sized comprehensive schools, for printing of the reports, administration, and governors' expenses. Attendance rates of parents at these meetings, nationwide, have been very small.

Heads, their staff and officers of the LEA are to be involved in the complexities of LMS, Local Management of Schools. The imposition of financial delegation, under LMS, and the consequent management time needed to administer a near-total budget for the school, will be considerable.

Recent approaches to industry–education links seem to place more faith in intentions than in either outcomes or the possibility to produce workable arrangements. There are cases, such as the Boston scheme and its imitator the London Compact, which seem to have had some success. It remains to be asked whether such schemes can be introduced with any national coherence. The time and effort required to find and organize industrial links is a severe and growing constraint on schools which seems not to have been questioned in terms of opportunity costs. Could the money and energy have been more productively employed elsewhere?

6 One or two measures, when judged alone, appear to have a fair degree of internal coherence and to be correctly targeted. However, in relation to other initiatives the

21

picture has a substantial lack of fit or incomplete linkage even in these cases.

A national curriculum was needed as a unifying force in British education. It, and its attendant assessment targets, constitute a fairly coherent initiative. At the implementation level, in the schools, this is to be introduced in parallel with TVE which will have an additional and sometimes complicating effect even though TVE, judged alone, could also be seen as a coherent package of measures. The emphasis in the national curriculum is upon individual subjects and defined standards, measured within these, of pupil attainment. The thrust of TVE is towards process and cross-curricular work, modular courses and multi-disciplinary skills. Both of them are diminished by the competition ethos generated by the government because both would be enhanced by local co-operation.

Britain and Japan are both island nations, each lying off the coast of a large and historically influential continent, our usable land areas are comparable in size and the opportunities available to both of us are similar. The economic progress of Japan since the end of the last war has been truly astounding whilst that of Britain has been slow and sporadic. A few facts and figures will be enough to gain an appreciation of Japan's achievement.

It has a Gross National Product (GNP) comprising 10 per cent of the world total, second only to that of the USA and is expected, by 1990, to have overtaken the USA in GNP per head of population and may even have taken the lead in absolute GNP by the turn of the century. Of the world's 34 largest banks 14 are Japanese but the Japanese Post Office savings deposits dwarf even those held in banks. The funds available for investment in industry are therefore immense. In 1987 Japan had a current account surplus of US$76 billion. Of companies with export sales in excess of US$1.5 billion annually, Japan has 20; the USA has 10. In the years 1979 to 1983 Japan lost about 3.5 million man-days due to industrial disputes; Britain lost about 54 million. The worst estimate of Japan's unemployment rate, using our method of calculation, is only half or less that in the UK. Japan has a steeply regressive tax system that results in greater equality of wealth. Consumer prices in Japan, for the period 1975–83, rose by 50 per cent; in Britain by 150 per cent.

Japan has the world's highest literacy rate despite having the world's most cumbersome and difficult writing system. Life expectancy in Japan is higher than in any other nation. The crime rate is the lowest – homicide is half our figure, rape is less than a quarter and robbery is less than $\frac{1}{23}$ of our rate. For the impact the Japanese economy has on the ordinary lives of British citizens I invite you to count the Japanese goods you own. Apart from the obvious high-cost items like cars, electronic goods, cameras, watches, typewriters, computers, and microwave ovens, look at small items like propelling pencils, ballpens, crockery, and so on. In crucial industries like the manufacture of digitally controlled machine tools, semi-conductors, and very large-scale integrated circuits, Japan is moving into first place. Research into the fifth-generation computer is thought to be ahead of the rest of the world.

Most of all, Japan is well on the way to developing a 'learning culture'. There is a general acceptance that learning, education, and training are lifelong activities. Part of this attitude, I believe, arises from the recognized exigencies of a rapidly changing world and the opportunities and problems with which it confronts individuals and societies. Part of it must be an outgrowth of a high standard of general education that promotes not only the capacity to continue lifetime education but is also its motivating progenitor.

It is not an idea I should like to pursue too far but, in some senses, Britain has as much to learn from the Japan of the 1960s and 1970s as from modern Japan. The problem we face now, the economic regeneration of the country, is the problem Japan tackled during earlier decades. We have the advantage, however, of hindsight in the Japanese experience. Their example tells us some of the problems we are likely to have to surmount or at least to bear. The price the Japanese people paid for their economic recovery was not cheap. The aphorism, 'the Japanese were poor people living in a rich country', had a strong element of truth even in the quite recent past. In some parts of Japan it may even be true today.

There has been failure to learn from the Japanese example that arises from a number of sources. Western thinking has shaped the modern world, including Japan. This has predisposed us to be teachers but not students; we give to the world but we do not receive from it. When the West seeks exemplars of good practice it looks shortsightedly inward at its own kind. The memory of empire, and the attitudes this bred into the British viewpoint, produces, perhaps, an especially severe myopia.

The second impediment to learning from Japan is of much more recent origin. It began in the 1960s when it was first realized how quickly Japan was catching up. It grew in the 1970s and had us wringing our hands in despair in the early 1980s. It is the belief that Japanese success depends on some strange quirk of the Japanese character that is so arcane, to them, that we cannot comprehend, let alone imitate it. It believes in a strange amalgam of half-understood notions and images of Japan. Businessmen and samurai, geisha and housewives, kamikaze pilots and workers seem to have fused to form the modern Japanese – creatures prepared to offer selfless devotion to the national cause and who have at their disposal semi-magical powers of subtlety, endurance, and cunning. This is a wrong view.

Most of the attributes that contribute to present-day Japanese success are post-war institutions, implemented not as a result of some strange cultural quirk but by rational decision making. This applies just as much to the lifetime employment system as it does to single-enterprise unions. It is true of the structure of the education system and the techniques of manufacturing in Japanese industry (see Chapter 8). Indeed, most of the 'magic' attributes of the Japanese turn out to be nothing of the kind. They are simply sensible ways of doing things – in that respect many of them are imitable by, or adaptable to, Britain.

The third obstacle is distinctly of our own making. It has, at heart, the British sense of fair play. When people wish, for whatever reason, to say something derogatory about the Japanese, they seize upon what is the best known fact about them. That is, throughout their history, they have been great copiers. They have not achieved their success by fair methods, we believe, and so do not deserve it.

This is a thoughtless disparagement. The British dislike of copying arises, in part, from a linguistic confusion. In schools, copying from someone else's work is treated as a heinous crime. 'Copy-cat' is one of the insults hurled around the classroom and the playground. 'Copy' and 'cheat' have become synonymous in the English language. The Japanese haven't just copied, they have cheated. Their route to economic supremacy hasn't been 'cricket'.

After the war the Japanese had urged upon them, by the occupying forces, an American model for their education system. They are now better educated than the Americans. This is 'American quantity, European quality' (Kahn 1971). If Daley's cartoon is as accurate as I suspect it is, however, Kahn must be referring to the French and the German education systems unless he means that tiny part of the British system that comprises higher education.

Modern communications have made Japan, and the rest of the world, our near neighbours. The developed nations are coming closer together; something approaching a world culture in attitudes is developing. The interchange this can accomplish, in ideas, in goods and in improvements to man's lot, can only be hindered by attitudes of superiority by one nation towards another; by the importance attached to skin colour; by the refusal to learn from one another. Japan has a great deal to offer Britain if we are not too proud to take it.

In the area of education this book will attempt to highlight what, in the current wave of change, is likely to succeed and what to fail. To do this, several perspectives will be taken. The first, and perhaps the most superficial, will be to seek a workable parallel in Japan. If such exists, to what degree is it successful and why? The second approach will ask what, in the Japanese package, will still be missing when our new initiatives have been implemented. In this case one must ask whether similar things could usefully be included in our systems or not. Clearly those rooted deep in Japan's unique culture will be unlikely candidates for importation. Others, we shall see, are logical outcomes of the same economic pressures faced by all nations of the developed world. They are rational decisions that, even if not part of the British system, often find counterparts in other countries responding to the same global needs. The third perspective is perhaps the most difficult to handle. What, in the British initiatives, is missing from Japanese systems? We must ask why we have made such inclusions in our set of changes and why Japan believes it can do without them.

A number of yardsticks will be used when making judgements. Due homage will be paid, certainly in the realm of education as opposed to training, to the desirability of education for its own sake. This is a subjective issue but an important one. Indeed, though I shall not labour the point, the improvement education produces in people, a truth I hold to be self-evident, is my personal major professional concern. That greater education produces greater economic progress I believe is true though I cannot prove it. It is an issue that I regard as the indispensable partner to 'education for its own sake'. It is a strong motivator of the changes the government is implementing. Thus, more objectively, I shall attempt to assess elements in education in the context of their likely impact on the nature of society and on economic performance. It will be generally assumed that, for the next several decades, Japan will be our, and everyone else's, major world competitor. In that sense, the potential of an initiative in education or training to enhance our competitiveness will be rated for its congruence with the government's objectives.

An important factor that will have to be taken into account is the 'Japanization' of British Industry. There are those who question whether this term has any meaning or not. I recognize two simple, and I think largely uncontroversial dimensions of 'Japanization'. The first is the presence of Japanese subsidiaries in Britain. These are likely to continue their proliferation, will become substantial employers of British workers and will have increasing effect on the firms that supply them. The recent EC 'anti-screwdrivering' laws will force Japanese firms to use larger percentages of locally (EC) produced components rather than importing them from Japan for assembly here. It is typically the case that large Japanese companies take a keen interest in the working practices of their suppliers and produce changes – 'Japanization' – in these firms. Our education and training systems will have to respond to the needs of those who will be working in Japanese companies or for suppliers operating under the demands of these companies.

A more controversial element in the term 'Japanization' is that relating to firms attempting to import Japanese methodologies. It is probably true to say that, at present, there is not a single firm that has imported the 'whole operating set' of a typical large Japanese company. It is equally likely that this would be an impossibility at present. However, many companies have imported elements of the Japanese set. Quality circles have been attempted with varying degrees of success: just-in-time (Toyota or *kanban*) systems are being tried. Single-union agreements may be a possible foreshadow of the Japanese 'single enterprise union'. If our economic future depends on learning from Japan, and importing her methods in the industrial and commercial sectors, we are forced to consider whether our education and training systems are congruent with this need.

2

The statistics of difference

Before we take our discussion any further it might be as well to make some assessment of the differences in educational standards in the two countries. This can in part be done by some international statistical comparisons. A fuller treatment of these can be obtained from the relevant literature. I shall touch briefly on a number of surveys conducted since the Second World War.

THE 1967 INTERNATIONAL STUDY OF ACHIEVEMENT IN MATHEMATICS

The study (Husen 1967) concerned itself with the mathematical abilities of 13- and 18-year-old students in 12 countries. The part of the survey yielding the clearest conclusions related to the 13-year olds (see Table 2.1). A set of 70 internationally agreed questions was put to random samples of pupils in each country (3,200 in England and Wales and 2,050 in Japan). Other data collected related to teachers, pupil attitudes, etc. Two sets of results were presented. The first consisted of the mean scores and standard deviations for the 13-year-old pupils in each country. The second set was for the school age group to which most 13-year olds belonged and thus would contain some 12-and 14-year olds. (In Japan the same pupils were used in both samples, hence figures are the same.) England/Wales and Scotland represent Britain.

Japanese children came out top in the first sample and second in the second sample where they were just beaten by Israeli youngsters (who were not represented in the first sample. The Israeli children in the second sample were 6 months older than

Table 2.1 Means and standard deviations in mathematics

Country (rank order 13-year olds)	13-year olds		School year group	
	Mean	SD	Mean	SD
1 Japan	31.2	16.9	31.2	16.9
5 England/Wales	19.3	17.0	23.8	18.5
6 Scotland	19.1	14.6	22.3	15.7
8 United States	16.2	13.3	17.8	13.3
9 Sweden (last)	15.7	10.9	15.3	10.8
All countries	overall		overall*	
	19.8	14.9	23.0	15.0

Source: Extract from Husen (1967), adapted from Lynn (1988)

* Includes figures for Germany, Finland, and Israel who participated only in School Year Group test

the Japanese). The difference in Japanese and English children's mean scores was 11.9 points on the first survey which is 0.8 of one overall standard deviation. Translated into percentages this means that 79 per cent of the Japanese children obtained higher scores than the average child in England – if they had been of the same competence only 50 per cent would have done so.

The figures for standard deviations from the mean are also eloquent. The size of the standard deviation in comparison with the mean reflects the variability of the scores the children achieved both above and below the mean. The English figures show a very large standard deviation (88 per cent of the mean in the first sample and nearly 78 per cent in the second) showing a very wide range of discrepancy in what the pupils could do. The Japanese standard deviation was only 54 per cent of the mean showing a much more uniform level of attainment. Deviation from the mean is not a worrying feature when applied to pupils achieving above the mean but must be one of great concern as it applies to underachievers. The high relative standard deviation, for British children, may echo our widespread tendency to teach courses that are differentiated, in content, difficulty, and teaching arrangements according to how the ability of pupils is perceived by their teachers rather than, as in Japan, setting a high expectation of all pupils and tending to ignore individual differences in ability when making the teaching provision. We should examine the possibility that this may be an inherent, and persistent, defect in British educational thinking.

Testing of 18-year olds presented more problems. There were wide discrepancies in the percentages of pupils staying on in school in the different countries. For example, in England only about 12 per cent, presumably the brightest, stayed on. In Japan, even in 1967, the figure was 57 per cent (now risen to 94 per cent). Furthermore the range of study varied widely. In England pupils were studying at most three A-levels, some of them specializing in mathematics, some doing none; in Japan pupils were doing nine subjects, some of them with a slight bias towards mathematics but all doing some (see 'Japanese national curriculum' in Chapter 5). The English mathematics specialists did better than those Japanese with a slight mathematical bias (mean of 35.2 against 31.4). The Japanese without a mathematical bias did better than the English non-mathematicians (25.3 against 21.40). These are not unexpected results until one recalls that over half of the age cohort was under test in Japan whilst in England only the brightest 12 per cent were involved.

When the top 4 per cent of those with a mathematical bias in Japan were compared with the best 4 per cent of mathematics specialists in England the results were surprising. The Japanese mean was 43.9 and the English 39.4 – the best Japanese 18-year olds, studying 9 subjects, were better in mathematics than the best specialists from England with only 3 subjects to contend with. When the top 3 per cent of Japanese, without any mathematical bias were compared with the top 3 per cent of English non-mathematicians the result was even more alarming (Japan mean of 51.7; England 30.2). The comparisons of the best 3 per cent and 4 per cent in the last two surveys are themselves oversimplifications. They represent, for England 3 per cent and 4 per cent of the best 12 per cent, the 'creme de la creme'; the Japanese were the top 3 per cent and 4 per cent of 57 per cent, a much more proletarian sample. In fact, in population terms, this means that, for non-maths specialists, the achievements of the top 3 per cent of Britain's 18-year olds were attained by only 36 people in 10,000.

In Japan the same or better attainment was reached by 171 per 10,000. For the British maths specialists, and those Japanese 18-year olds with a slight bias towards maths (best 4 per cent in each country) the equivalent top attainments were attained by 48 per 10,000 in Britain and 228 per 10,000 in Japan. Arguments for the retention of A-level, as a necessary pre-condition to the maintenance of academic excellence, would appear, from these comparisons with Japan, at least as far as mathematics is concerned, to be invalid. It would seem, in Japan, that the concentration of effort across the whole ability spectrum has done nothing to affect the achievements of the very brightest in a particular subject.

However, I recently had the benefit of hosting in my school a number of Japanese teachers, who were on an extended study visit to Britain. The mathematics specialist was surprised by the degree of difficulty at which A-level in the subject was taught. In his view this was higher than in Japan. Indeed the same comment was made about the whole range of A-level subjects by the study team. This inclines me to view with some scepticism the deductions above from the 1967 Husen survey. In Chapter 3 I shall be questioning the continued existence of A-level courses but my arguments do not depend upon the undoubtedly high level of attainment the examination expects.

In general it is fair to say that, on average, Japanese children at age 13 are achieving as well in mathematics as 16-year-old British children (Prais 1987). The vast majority of British children, at this age, are about to complete their mathematical education. The Japanese 13-year olds, at the same standard, *still have 6 more years of mathematical education in front of them* before they leave upper-secondary school. It is not difficult to discern the competitive edge this gives to Japanese industry. Even those who leave education at 18 constitute a very numerate workforce able to undertake, profitably, the training they will be given. They will be able to make an educated contribution to discussion in quality circles. They will be able to comprehend economic arguments as they affect their pay claims, company profitability, and the social structure of the nation.

THE INTERNATIONAL STUDY OF SCIENCE ACHIEVEMENT

This study (Comber and Keeves 1973; see Table 2.2) tested scientific factual recall, comprehension and application of principles and knowledge in novel contexts, in physics, chemistry, biology and earth sciences. It was administered to children of 10 and 14 years of age. Several thousand children were tested in each age range in each country. Japanese children came out on top in both age groups. The results confirm those in the 1967 mathematics test above. Although Japanese children did well in the recall of factual information they were not the highest scorers. What put them into first place was a superior ability to apply what they had learned. This is a point worth noting by those who assume that the Japanese do well when handling straight fact but are lacking in higher talents. There is a widely held belief amongst the Japanese themselves that their education system produces individuals lacking the capacity to apply intellect in new situations. The results of these tests might indicate their fears are exaggerated.

Table 2.2 Science achievement, 10- and 14-year olds

Country rank order 14-year olds	Rank order 10-year olds	10-year olds		14-year olds	
		Mean	SD	Mean	SD
1 Japan	1	21.7	7.7	31.2	14.8
7 United States	4	17.7	9.3	21.6	11.6
8 Scotland	11	14.0	8.4	21.4	14.2
9 England/Wales	8	15.7	8.5	21.3	14.1
14 Belgium (FR) (last)	12	13.9	7.1	15.4	8.8
All countries		overall		overall	
		16.7	7.9	22.3	11.8

Source: Extract from Comber and Keeves (1973)

Significant features worth note, once again, are revealed by the standard deviations compared with the means. For 14-year-old Japanese children the SD is just under 50 per cent of the mean. British children show a much greater spread in attainment, the SD is about 66 per cent of the mean. In fact, when we run our eyes down the extreme right-hand column of the table the outstanding feature is the sudden rise in SD for both Scotland, England and Wales. Our primary school 10-year olds, however, have SDs much more in line with those of other countries, clustered around 50 per cent of the mean. Our primary school children, taught largely in mixed-ability classes, show a much smaller spread in ability than do our 14-year olds. Could these figures once again reveal that our preoccupation with teaching courses, differentiated according to how schools perceive the ability of children may be misguided? (see Chapter 5).

THE 1980s (SECOND) INTERNATIONAL STUDY OF ACHIEVEMENT IN MATHEMATICS

Perhaps the most alarming feature of this study (Garden, not yet published in full; see Table 2.3) relates to those 'anchor questions' that were common to both the 1960s and 1980s studies in the ten countries that participated in both tests. There was some decline in the standards of pupils in all countries, according to the National Curriculum Working Group for Mathematics (DES 1988); however, the decline for England and Wales was the largest and was the only one in which a decline was present in all branches of the subject:

it must be a matter of concern that the overall performance of English pupils is not more distinguished, and that the substantial changes in school curricula in mathematics in England in this period have not borne an obvious fruit when judged by internationally agreed standards.

(Prais 1987)

Table 2.3 The 1980s international study of achievement in mathematics (Garden, not yet published in full)

Figures for 13-year olds

Country	Mean score %
England	48.61
Scotland	49.67
Japan	64.57
All countries	mean of means 51.80

Source: Adapted from Lynn, op. cit.

The National Curriculum Working Group for Mathematics gives the explanation a slightly more comforting slant: 'since the 1960s, the content and style of mathematics teaching has changed, making some of the test items used, which test a narrow range of skills, less appropriate' (p. 5, item 3.8).

We cannot avoid asking the question – if the test items were 'less appropriate' why were they chosen to test international standards? We can only judge their validity if we know what the questions were. Fortunately the working group gives us examples and results for British pupils (Table 2.4). I can see nothing inappropriate in this type of question and echo the working group's alarm. Only a little over a third of pupils were able to indicate the correct answer of 2.55. Almost a third selected an answer that was outside the range of the numbers in question (7.65) indicating a total incomprehension of the principles of averaging – many would seem simply to have added the numbers. It is worth bearing in mind, also, that in a multiple-choice question with five choices, 20 per cent of the pupils could get the correct answer by random selection. One must speculate on how many could have produced a reasonable answer if they had had to work it out for themselves.

Table 2.4 Anchor question in mathematics test: British children

The arithmetic average of 1.50, 2.40, 3.75 is equal to	% of pupils giving each answer 1964	1981
A 2.40	3	10
B 2.55	51	36
C 3.75	3	4
D 7.65	26	31
E none of these	11	14

Source: National Curriculum Working Group for Mathematics (1988)

Is Sig Prais hinting, in his comment above, at the 'intentions as surrogates for outcomes' fallacy that is so prevalent in British education? The clear intention of various movements to 'improve' standards in mathematics, by the ready acceptance of new approaches to the subject, has conspicuously lacked measurement of outcomes in terms of what pupils can do. It is substantially true, of British education in general, that if the *intentions* of a reformatory movement are in the right direction, and the new theory on which it is based has a pleasing enough ring to it and is buttressed with some appropriate philosophy, then it is is liable to attract a sympathetic hearing. Whether or not its aims are realized in practice is often a secondary, or at least late, consideration. British education has been remarkably prone to adhere to 'the beautiful theory' in the face of 'the ugly fact'.

The television programme *Educating Britain* presented a German mathematics test paper to equivalent children in the British age and ability spectrum. Our results were substantially worse than those of the Germans as we have come to expect in international comparisons. Asked to comment on this, an educationalist criticized the mechanical form in which the questions had been presented. She pointed out that in Britain we teach pupils to understand the nature of a problem and to grasp the mathematical ideas behind it. What she actually meant was this is the intention of our methodology. Both groups were set the sort of test she would have preferred. Again the German pupils did much better than ours; they were also able to point out the principles behind their answers. Our children's performance had not improved on that in the mechanical test.

The importance of this television item, for me, was not the validity, or otherwise, of a small sample test conducted by the production team but the readiness with which the British educator was able to find solace and refuge in the appeal to intentions which turned out, in this case, to be wholly illusory. The item made a direct appeal to my memories of many similarly irritating encounters with complacency.

Other studies confirm the comparative high performance of the Japanese education system. The interested reader is referred to the Sendai−Minneapolis−Taipei Study (Stigler *et al.* 1982) and the Illinois−Japan Study of Mathematics (Walberg, Harnisch, and Tsai 1985).

SURVEYS OF INFLUENTIAL FACTORS

The National Curriculum Working Group for Mathematics (DES 1988) refers to the factors that are likely to account for the differences in standards between Japan and Britain:

> The Japanese system of education, the level of provision for mathematics and the content of the mathematics curriculum, are all heavily influenced by the attitudes, expectations and aspirations of the Japanese people, all of which appear very different from those which exist in the UK.
>
> (p. 112, item 49)

In this section I shall attempt to address some of these differences in a statistical form. More detail on the organization of the British and Japanese education system generally appears in later chapters.

Attitudes: Tables 2.5 and 2.6

Later in the book I shall refer to British observers who point to the didactic and, by our standards, uninteresting nature of the teaching in Japanese schools. This is a point of view with which I concur unreservedly. I should be worried to find any of my own staff teaching in this style. Equally I must recognize the possibility that this is a *teacher's* view. It is coloured by the dominant ethos of the profession from which I would find it hard to escape. I must also recognize that a child's view of what constitutes a good lesson or what objectively is a good lesson may not accord with this view.

The attitude questionnaire that yielded the results in Table 2.5 asked pupils whether they liked school, wanted to get as good an education as possible, and so on. It would seem that Japanese children were, at the very least, prepared to tolerate the teaching methods. Could it be significant that, on every measure above, Britain, a strong proponent of innovative *and child centred* teaching styles, seemed to accomplish little in generating favourable attitudes in its pupils? The magnitude of discrepancy in the table is not large. One could not say from these results that pupils in Japan were a great deal more inspired to work hard than their British counterparts. However, if we consider that the decline in British mathematical standards mentioned above is hardly likely to be indicative of any improvement in attitude of pupils between the 1967 measures of standards and attitudes and the present, certain doubts must spring to mind.

We have put immense thought and heart-searching into new styles of teaching, all with the specific intention of capturing the pupils' interest. It is worth considering whether or not, at best,

Table 2.5 Mean scores on attitude to school work

Country rank order 13-year olds	13-year olds	18-year old maths specialists	rank order	18-year old non-maths specialists	rank order
1 Japan	10.5	10.6	1	11.4	1
6 England/Wales	9.3	8.5	7	8.5	6
7 Scotland	9.1	9.7	5	8.5	6
8 United States (last)	8.4	8.0	8	8.3	8

Source: Adapted from Husen (1967)

this has been a waste of time; at worst, counter-productive. Have we deluded ourselves by assuming that because teachers think a new style should be more interesting that it is so to the pupils? All teachers will be familiar with that, to us, depressing class whose greatest joy in life seems to be a double period of notetaking and which has resisted, with stolid implacability, all our efforts to vary the educational diet.

The 1973 international study of attainment in science also investigated attitudes to school in 10- and 14-year olds. The results, in Table 2.6 are given as standard scores around a mean of 0.

Table 2.6 Attitudes to school: science, 10- and 14-year olds

Country	10-year olds	Rank	14-year olds	Rank
Japan	+ 19	2	+ 20	2
United States	+ 14	3	+ 19	3
England/Wales	+ 5	5	+ 7	5
Scotland	+ 5	5	+ 3	7

Source: Adapted from Comber and Keeves (1973)

The survey again puts Japan near the top in pupil attitude. The discrepancies are not as large as they might appear owing to the peculiarities of a standard distribution method of presentation. Britain improves its position to above the middle of the league. Could this be a marginal reflection, I wonder, of the move towards comprehensive education that gathered momentum during the period between the Husen and the Comber and Keeves surveys?

Curriculum coverage: Table 2.7

An important determinant of how a nation's children perform in international tests is, of course, the degree to which the internationally defined question content has been covered in the nation's teaching. Estimates of coverage were made by teachers in the different countries. In maths this is presented as a percentage, in science as an index of coverage. The investigators found high correlations between the degree of coverage and the results of the pupils sitting the tests (0.64 for maths and 0.80 for science).

Table 2.7 Coverage of test material in the schools

Country	Maths	Rank	Science	Rank
Japan	63.1	2	296	1
England/Wales	60.4	3	179	11
Scotland	51.3	7	190	7
Sweden	37.4	8 (lowest)	188	8
Netherlands	–	–	137	13 (lowest)

Source: Adapted from Husen (1967) and Comber and Keeves (1973)

In mid 1960s, the date of the maths tests, there was little real debate, in Britain, about what ought to be taught in a maths curriculum. This was pretty well nationally agreed. Furthermore, all pupils studied mathematics, to some level, throughout school life. Indeed, there is little difference between the coverage of the test material in Japan and in Britain. There is nothing here, then, to account for the difference in performance. The situation in science was very different even in the 1970s when the science tests were conducted. The teaching style, curriculum, organizational content and objectives were much more at the discretion of individual schools. Many British pupils drop science at an early stage or have incomplete coverage. To this day science in primary schools is a sketchily undertaken activity. We should expect to find a low index of coverage when compared with Japan operating a tight national curriculum.

Teacher ability and qualification: Table 2.8

Passow *et. al.* found no correlation between teachers' pay and the 1976 attainments of children in science at either 10 or 14 years of age. However, Husen gives a correlation of minus 0.87 between the attainments of 13-year olds in maths and teachers' pay. If this is an accurate reflection of reality, children do better in countries where the teachers' pay is lower. Not wishing to be dismembered by my own profession, I would hasten to add that there are other and good reasons for paying teachers well. I simply make the point that, on this evidence, it does not lead to high pupil attainment.

For our purposes, it will be seen that there is a high similarity between England/Wales and Japan as far as length of tertiary education and pay are concerned. To the extent that anything

Table 2.8 Teacher comparisons

Country	Ability Rating (1)		Length Tertiary (2)		Pay Indices (3)		
	prim.	sec.	prim.	sec.	prim.	sec.	all
England/Wales	A	—	2.3	3.3	86	51	80
Italy	BA	BA	1.1	4.2	67	42	100
Scotland	A	AA	3.2	4.3	—	—	120
Japan	AA	A	2.7	3.7	86	57	78

Sources: 1 and 3, Passow *et al.* (1976): 2, Comber and Keeves (1973)
Key:
1 A = average; BA = below average; AA = above average (entrants)
2 Figures relate to average length of tertiary education of teachers
3 Primary teachers' pay as % minor white-collar workers; secondary teachers' pay as % of major professional workers; all teachers' pay as % of average earnings in manufacturing industry

can be deduced from Passow's ability rating, Japanese primary school teachers are rated slightly higher than ours. The high scoring, on all counts of teachers in Scotland, does not seem, when we examine the table on pupil attainment, to have produced the result one would have expected. The difference between England/Wales and Scotland is slight; the attainment of Scottish children is substantially lower than that of the Japanese. There is a correlation of 0 between the length of primary school teachers' education and attainment of children on the international science tests for 10-year olds and no significant correlations, either positive or negative, between the length of education of secondary school teachers and attainment of pupils on tests for 13-year olds in maths and 14-year olds in science (Lynn 1988).

Spending on schools and pupils: Table 2.9

Since we have failed to find the answer to the discrepancy between Japanese attainment and ours in the quality and pay of teachers, it may be worth looking to see how well the schools are financed.

The first three columns of Table 2.9 show that the per capita expenditure on Japanese pupils in 1967 was very low compared with ours. Husen found negative correlations statistically significant at the 5 per cent level for the 13-year olds and 18-year-old non-maths between expenditure and attainment over a range of ten countries. In straight language, the pupils in the nations spending less were doing better.

Table 2.9 Expenditure on pupils and education service (selected countries)

| Country | Expenditure per pupil $US | | | Expenditure on education % of GNP |
	13-year olds	18-year maths	18-year non-maths	
England/Wales	208	237	235	5.8
Japan	53	80	65	5.8
France	197	308	288	5.0
United States	214	270	270	7.0
Netherlands	154	357	356	8.4
Sweden	227	263	265	9.5

Source: Pupil expenditures: Husen (1967): *United Nations Demographic Year Book*, adapted from Lynn

In expenditure related to Gross National Product (GNP) the nations studied fell into two groups of which samples are shown in the table. Both Britain and Japan fell into the low spending group with the same proportion of GNP dedicated to education. Again we fail to find a reason for Japan's better performance.

The sizes of classes and the pupil/teacher ratio of schools: Table 2.10

In the minds of educators and the perception of the general public it has become axiomatic that small class size leads directly to better teaching. This is a major negotiating point that the teaching unions take to the government. Pay teachers more, attract more of them, reduce class sizes, provide better education – is the cycle of argument. We have seen this cycle broken at the point of teachers' pay. Our evidence fails to make the connection between more pay and better education. What about reduction in class size?

The only results here, for the whole range of countries considered, that were statistically significant at the 5 per cent level for correlations between size and attainment were for 18-year-old non-maths specialists and 14-year-old (secondary) science

(0.62 and 0.59 respectively). In other words, the larger the class size or number of pupils per teacher, the better the pupils did in the tests. This is a direct contradiction of the conventional wisdom.

Table 2.10 Class sizes and pupil/teacher ratios of schools

Country	Size of teaching class			P/T ratio (school) x:1 (science tests 1973)	
	13-year olds	18-year maths	18-year non-maths	primary	secondary
England/Wales	30	12	22	28.4	18.0
Scotland	30	21	22	27.4	17.1
United States	29	21	26	25.5	19.7
Japan	41	41	41	27.4	21.9

Source: Husen (1967): Comber and Keeves (1973), adapted from Lynn

I am sceptical about the figures for the size of non-maths classes for 18-year olds in Britain. These relate, presumably, to all sixth-form classes other than mathematics in the mid-1960s. It seems to me that half or less of the figure given would have been a more accurate reflection of reality.

Perhaps the figures for 13-year-old classes are the most indicative of the difference in size of teaching groups. Japanese classes are very much larger than ours. It can be seen from the pupil–teacher ratios for schools that the overall staffing differences are slight compared with the differences in class sizes. This apparent contradiction is resolved by consideration of the contact ratio – the fraction of the working week that a teacher spends in front of a class. In Britain this is high. It is common for secondary teachers to have perhaps only four or five preparation periods in a week of 40 periods. In primary schools the contact ratio is even higher – indeed it is not unusual for a teacher to spend the entire week in front of the class. The high contact ratio is the price we pay for having smaller classes. Japanese teachers spend much less time in front of the class and can use the rest of the time for preparation, marking, pastoral work and so on. Japanese teachers of my acquaintance estimate their no-contact time at about a third of the teaching week. The trade-off, in this case, is larger classes. It would seem from the statistics that Japan's is the better of the two options. Furthermore, in the presently hectic climate generated by the educational reforms, it may be doubly important to give teachers less contact time. It is a common view of heads that their staffs are nearing the point of collapse under the deluge of change heaped upon them. If the reforms are to be effected properly, teachers need time to prepare new schemes, to train themselves and to consult with one another.

The realities of operating a high contact ratio can be severe. Research has shown that the stress level of classroom teaching is higher than in almost any other job. Simply being under the eye of an audience of thirty watchful children increases heart rate and blood pressure. The strain of attempting to give up to eight good 'performances' a day can cause severe strain on the teacher. I have seen strong men and determined women visibly weakened by an 8-period teaching day. For my own part, I admit freely to a tailing off (or rapid decline!) in my ability to perform for the class in the days when I was subjected to a full teaching time-table. Is it worth considering at least an experiment in some schools to see whether a smaller contact ratio, and larger classes, would lead to better education and improved standards? It may well be, considering all the other tasks, new styles of delivery, and in-service training expected under the current round of change, that this may be the only feasible option. Even the best teachers have a finite amount of energy. Time they are prepared to devote outside school is not limitless.

THE LENGTH OF THE SCHOOL YEAR AND THE *JUKU*

1976 figures from Passow show that the Japanese school year of 240 days and 1,104 hours is much longer than our 180 days and 900 hours. (There were sinister rumours that Mr Baker intended to lengthen the school teaching day.) The difference does not end here, however. Many Japanese children attended *juku* – extra schooling institutions – during evenings, holidays and weekends. So competitive has the Japanese education system become that the growth of *juku* has been very rapid. Japan's National Institute for Educational Research found, in 1986, that attendance by 12- to 13-year olds, in different areas of the country ranged from 1.5 to 2.5 hours per week. A survey by the Ministry of Education showed that 16.5 per cent of primary pupils and 44.5 per cent of all junior high school pupils were attending *juku*. In Tokyo and other large centres of population, where *juku* provision is greatest, about 47 per cent of 11- to

12-year olds and 67 per cent of 14- to 15-year olds attended such institutions.

Juku have really only one function: to help pupils pass exams. They do not educate in the sense we and the Japanese understand the term. I make this distinction because the Japanese are an educated, not simply highly qualified, people. The existence of *juku* is often put forward as the reason why the Japanese do well in international tests. This may well be the case, there is not enough evidence either to confirm or refute this hypothesis. In my view, the *juku* have very little to do with the real standard of education of the Japanese as evidenced in the society and the workplace. The defining characteristic of the Japanese functioning in the latter is a high degree of adaptability and transferability of skills and knowledge, characteristics that are the antithesis of *juku* methods. Nor does the 'learning culture' which is so much in evidence in Japan seem to be a natural outgrowth of *juku* mentality (Drew 1986). Japan's 'learning culture' is explored more fully in later chapters.

To conclude this chapter I shall put aside the statistics in favour of two incidentals of Japanese school life which may be a more eloquent comment than a whole book of facts and figures. As is often the case, it is the seeming trivialities that most vividly encapsulate the grand design. They can seldom be quantified. If this chapter has any point, indeed, if the book has any point, these two trifles might well be my summary.

First, just inside the doorway of a Japanese school is an open space with shoe racks. The pupils change to indoor shoes as they enter the building, just as they do in Japanese homes, so as to avoid bringing in dirt. The school projects the image that it is just as worthy of respect as the home itself.

Second, it is the responsibility of children in a Japanese school to keep the place clean and tidy. Cleaners are not employed to perform this task. Typically the 'homeroom' (form) teacher helps and supervises. Sometimes the children work with more enthusiasm than effect and sometimes, in the case of individuals, neither is much in evidence. However, the general effect on the social fabric of the school is high. I am sure that this must go a long way towards inculcating the respect for the environment that also stops the Japanese throwing down litter in the streets. The message projected by these two features is that Japanese schools matter to the pupils.

This is in stark contrast with what happens in Britain. In many schools that I have visited the only way to remove litter is to form punishment squads of after-school detainees. It is a common feature of schools that pupils have to carry all their belongings, including their coats, with them, simply to avoid having them stolen. Vandalism, especially of toilet facilities, increasingly a crime perpetuated more by girls than by boys, is rampant. After-hours break-ins and, in many education authorities, arson by pupils of school buildings, are both on the increase. Truancy in schools, especially in the depressed areas and the inner cities, has reached crisis proportions (see Chapter 3).

Our schools, most of our pupils and our society deserve better.

3

Elements missing from the educational reforms

Anthony Crossland, as Secretary of State for Education, remarked that the nearest the cabinet had ever come to talking about education, during his tenure of office, was to discuss the Oxford ring-road (Kogan 1971). The high profile of government-sponsored educational change in the late 1980s is rather new to us. Since 1944 only the issues surrounding 'going comprehensive' have attracted so much public attention and hence succeeded in engaging the concern of politicians. The battlefield of change is, inevitably, in the areas where entrenched viewpoints and reformatory zeal coincide. It is not surprising then, that commentators should be able to point to elements they regard as missing from the package of change – ideas lost in the heat of battle; reforms that became casualities; conflicts that both sides avoided in the interests of good tactics. Judged in the light of comparison with Japan, certain obvious deficiencies spring to mind.

An education system can only be fairly judged, in the last analysis, on its outcome. Taken as a whole, in comparison with most of the developed world, we are a poorly educated people. This delivers the verdict on our system: it can and must do better. No amount of self-justifying rhetoric can avoid this conclusion. The impressive array of unfulfilled intentions of the past will do nothing to sustain our future; they merely draw the veil of complacency over our failure.

To extract, from an industrial world, a civilized and humanizing existence, requires a high standard of education, directly congruent with the economic culture, for the whole population. Without this, man becomes a drab slave of his own machines and systems. Unless the economic culture progresses, co-operates and competes with others of a similar kind it will find itself denied options others take for granted. As it falls behind it will become unstable because the expectations of the people are not being met; it will not be able to stand comparison, in the eyes of its own population, with societies that are doing better. This is likely to cause political instability.

These two criteria, the humanization of an industrial society and the economic progress that is required to sustain it, over-whelmingly argue the case for general education as the most important contribution that can be made towards progress. The raising up of one section at the expense of another will not serve either purpose. Given that human intelligence has been unfairly apportioned in the society, some will always be better educated than others but all must rise to the degree their potential admits.

That this has not normally been the case is the root of Britain's educational failure. In 1982 there were 650,000 pupils aged 16-plus who were entitled to leave school. Of these 100,000 had no qualifications at all, 300,000 had not enough to qualify for any further education (they had a few lower grade CSE subjects), 200,000 continued in post-16 education of some kind and only 50,000 went on to higher education; 250,000 became unemployed (Villiers 1984). In Britain only about 13 or 14 per cent of pupils go on to some form of higher education. In Germany and France 26 per cent and in Japan 40 per cent receive higher educa-tion. In Britain only about 40 per cent receive education beyond 16 years of age (see Table 3.1). It is difficult to produce figures that are easily compared internationally because of the pre-valence of part-time vocational education. In Japan 94 per cent continue post-compulsory education in school. According to a *Financial Times* survey in 1983 there were two million illiterate adults in Britain, 30 per cent of the population did not under-stand percentages and 60 per cent did not understand the meaning of 'rate' when applied to variables like inflation, growth and foreign exchange. 'Less than half of pupils leave school with a piece of paper that an employer is prepared to consider significant', according to Michael Young, Chairman of the Manpower Services Commission, in 1984.

The Japanese education system was reformed during the American occupation that followed the last war. It set itself one clear goal – the improvement of the educational standard of *the whole nation*. Arguably, this has been the most important contributor to Japan's economic boom in the post-war period.

Table 3.1 European staying-on rates

| Country | Years spent in formal education beyond compulsory schooling | | | |
	None %	1–3 %	4+ %	No reply %
Luxembourg	12	37	42	9
Germany	16	58	22	4
Netherlands	23	40	21	16
Greece	29	46	24	1
France	30	50	17	3
Belgium	30	43	17	10
Denmark	33	40	12	15
Ireland	34	50	11	5
Portugal	36	34	17	13
Italy	39	23	33	5
Spain	42	23	15	20
United Kingdom	60	30	6	4

Source: Adapted from TES 3.3.89

Britain's relative economic failure can, in contrast, be described in terms of the failure of the education system to provide the bulk of the population with the necessary intellectual apparatus to make the nation competitive in the modern world. Although Britain far outstrips Japan, and most of the rest of the world, in producing inventors and Nobel prize winners we have failed at the more mundane levels of the ability spectrum. There is gross underdevelopment in the general education of the people who will become the workforce, the technicians, the engineers and managers, where invention and discovery can be capitalized upon to the benefit of economic growth. Perhaps, more importantly, the relative untrainability of the British workforce has been our major impediment. Comparisons of manufacturing techniques in the kitchen furniture industry revealed that German workers were capable of getting the best out of sophisticated machinery and flexible production systems. German manufacturers have been able to move quickly to fill the growing demand for up-market 'customization'. British firms were trapped at the low end of the market where, because of inadequate development in the workforce, new techniques were often merely devices to deskill or replace workers. Production was confined to the low end of the market where simple mass production of standard units was the norm (Steedman and Wagner 1987). This unfavourable contrast is repeated so often in comparison with the Japanese workforce as to require little further comment. Blame for the unfavourable position of Britain in such comparisons can be laid squarely on the education system as the primary point of failure and secondly on inadequate efforts in training.

An imperative of adaptation to the pace of change in the modern world is an education sufficient to comprehend the options and possibilities:

the future long-term economic performance of an organisation is linked with its capacity to anticipate and respond to uncertainty and change in its environment . . . [and this] . . . will demand that organisations, whether public or private, position themselves for uncertainty. This in turn has implications for the capabilities of all who work for the enterprise. . . . The whole workforce will need to be able to learn how to make creative contributions as well as being able to make them in practice.

(Fonda and Hayes 1988)

The education system was, in the past, and is still to a significant degree, a chief contributor to class divisions. Through these divisions the 'two sides' of industry, and their accompanying syndrome of economic ills, are perpetuated. Our education system not only fails, relatively, to equip a large percentage of school leavers with adequate intellectual skills but is relatively unable, compared with many of our competitors, to engender an industrial relations climate in which change is possible and progress can be made.

It appears to me, that the general problem in British education is the lack of structural coherence capable of providing motivators at all levels of ability. Put crudely, the system is full of holes through which far too many pupils are able to drop. It is from those features of the Japanese education system that enhance motivation that we have most to learn. I shall pay scant regard to intrinsic motivation because, while recognizing its importance, it is so bound up with cultural values that it is difficult to propose lessons that could be learned from Japan. The topic is briefly treated by Lynn (1988).

The extrinsic motivators that are structured into the Japanese education system are, however, well worth consideration in the light of Britain's current round of educational reforms. The organization of education and the value placed by employers on general educational standard in Japan provide a high level of motivating incentives for the system as a whole to perform well (see Chapter 4). These operate at many levels – for the child, the teacher, the school. In Britain the part played by structural incentives in education is almost unconsidered. Little regard is paid to them in educational literature, in courses for teachers, in the schools and in national reviews.

Nowhere, perhaps, is the problem of low motivation and the lack of structural incentives more manifest, for the majority of children, than in our low take-up of education beyond compulsory schooling. I shall consider this in the next section as typifying the ways in which the British system tends to demotivate by erecting systems that act as disincentives for the bulk of the school population however much they may motivate the most able.

In a very real sense I regard the achievement of continued education beyond 16-plus to be the most central issue of Britain's current failure, the seminal problem for educational reform. If for no other reason, it is the indispensable first step to the development of a 'learning culture' throughout the age range of the population – for the young in preparation for life, for the workforce in adaptation to the rapidly changing needs of employment, for the aged to enhance the years after work. For all of us, the growth of a 'learning culture' must be the response to the acceleration in technology and its social and economic change.

GENERAL STAYING-ON BEYOND COMPULSORY SCHOOLING

a little more than one half leave school for the labour market at age sixteen. . . . For this group, the goal of general education to age eighteen (which most could expect to obtain if they lived in Japan or Taiwan) seems unrealistic, without fundamental structural change unlikely to be achieved in the next two decades.

(White 1988)

The combination of poor performance during the compulsory schooling years and a high percentage of students leaving school at 16 has meant that the average English worker enters employment with a relatively low level of qualification.

(Finegold and Soskice 1988)

Whatever comparisons we make between our education system and that of Japan, whether we believe, at the end of the day, that we can learn anything from Japan, one startling difference must be confronted squarely. Nearly all Japanese are educated to the age of 18, about 94 per cent of the population passing through the schools, a figure about twice as high as the best estimates for Britain. There is a quantity of education that we are unable to match. The quality of Japanese education as far as it is amenable to objective measurement has been discussed in the previous chapter.

The British education system grew piecemeal through various education acts and never really managed to shake itself free from a type of thinking derived from the class sytem. The old divisions into public, grammar, and secondary modern schools were as much reflections of money, class and status as they were of educational ability. Of course, an unrepresentative proportion of working-class children were able to enter the grammar schools but frequently they were confronted by an alien milieu that inhibited progress and their success rate was even less representative of their numbers in the population (Jackson and Marsden 1962). Even today banding and streaming systems within comprehensive schools perpetuate, but mercifully to a slighter degree, the same divisions. True to this form, education beyond 16 is designed for elites (see Chapter 7). 'English deficiencies in education, the mass exodus at 16, the narrow funnel which rations higher education, the peculiar English notion that half of the nation is best served by plunging into employment, unemployment or a low-grade youth training scheme at 16' (TES 23.9.88).

The Japanese education system aims at a good general education, in a broad range of subjects, up to the age of 18. Schools are organized on a 6–3–3 system in which a child spends the first 6 years of schooling, up to the age of 12, in primary school followed by 3 years in each of a lower secondary and an upper-secondary school. I shall be returning to discussion of the lower/upper secondary split later on. The organization of the system and the ranking of and admission to upper-secondary schools also act as strong incentives in their own right (see Chapter 4 on examination systems and progression routes). Compulsory education, in fact, ends at the age of 15 with the completion of lower secondary. In practice, however, 94 per cent of pupils go on to the next optional stage, upper-secondary school. This is a stark contrast with the situation in Britain where more than half of pupils leave education at 16-plus and, in comparison with Japan, constitute thereafter, an under-educated segment of our society.

Perhaps important, in separating cultural attributes from pragmatic systems, is a consideration of the post-war changes in continued education in Britain and Japan. Japan has shown faster growth than Britain which started from a higher base. This seems to me to argue that there is nothing intrinsically Japanese in a high take up of continued education but that Japanese structures have responded suitably to a changing world in promoting this uptake. Table 3.2 seems to indicate that other nations have also shown a more rapid response than Britain, a further indicator that the difference is not culture-dependent but arises from the organization of the systems. It is worth noting that, because the figures relate to averages of the entire population aged 15 to 64 in each year of measurement, there is a considerable damping effect on the differences revealed. For example, many of those falling into the 1950 statistic would still count and depress the measures in 1984. As these fall out of the samples in the future, we should expect a very rapid acceleration of Japanese figures compared with Britain's.

Table 3.2 Average years of secondary education for population aged 15–64 in 1950, 1973, and 1984

Country (rank order 1984)	Secondary			% increase 1950 to 1984	Rank order increase
	1950	1973	1984		
West Germany	4.37	5.11	5.17	18.3	6
USA	3.40	4.62	5.10	50.0	4
France	3.04	4.11	4.89	60.8	3
Japan	2.08	3.79	4.56	119.2	2
Britain	3.27	3.99	4.50	37.6	5
Netherlands	1.17	2.49	3.34	185.4	1

Source: Adapted from Maddison (1987)

Conspicuously absent from the current spate of educational reforms, is the question about how to reduce our deficit in staying-on rates. We might have begun to tackle this question when the new GCSE 16-plus examinations were mooted. We might have wondered if there is any inherently significant reason to regard 16-plus as a natural termination of education for most of the population. The problem has been addressed very peripherally. The provision has shifted from education to training; resources have gone to YTS rather than schools. YTS in fact offers a financial incentive to young people to abandon full-time education. The government seems confused about how, structurally, the education system can be made to motivate students (White 1988). We have turned our faces away from education at just the moment in a youngster's life when the social adult is beginning to form. We begin, instead, training or employment whilst the raw material is still, educationally, very incomplete.

It is important to note that most upper-secondary schools in Japan broadly continue, and develop, the work of general education begun in lower-secondary schools. Education continues on a wide front and narrow specialization is avoided. There are some upper-secondary institutions that have a technical or vocational slant but the number of pupils opting for such courses is small, around 30 per cent, the majority preferring the general courses (see Chapters 5, 6, and 7). Even in the vocational high schools, half of the curricular time is spent on general subjects.

Generally, in Britain, education beyond compulsory level, in schools, and the courses available, are dominated by the Advanced-level examinations: 'an educational ethos dominated by the demands of [entry to] higher education as expressed through the public examination system, and geared, through early specialisation, towards producing a small academic elite' (TES 23.9.88).

This merely perpetuates the historical situation in which public and grammar school pupils were the ones who stayed on after compulsory schooling. The remainder, perhaps 60 per cent or more, were expected to leave school and find work. It could be argued, though I don't believe it, that the education the lower-ability levels received was sufficient for them to cope with the world as it was two or three decades ago. To cling to this notion in the present day is to base our educational provision on a total misconception of needs of people in a high-tech era. We no longer live in a world where the employment of hewers of wood and drawers of water constitute the bulk need of our society. There has been a quantum leap forward in the need for prolonged general education.

A-LEVEL: THE FOCUS OF EDUCATIONAL INCOHERENCE

Britain has done little to promote the staying-on rate of all but the brightest pupils. There are some courses now available in schools, for the non-A-level pupil who stays on beyond 16, but even here the main provision, the Certificate of Pre-Vocational Education, seems to be shifting towards a training-orientated ethos (TES 16.12.88). The bias, at the school level, of educational priorities and the allocation of resources, is still towards the A-level candidates and the potential entrants to higher education.

Before we begin to consider some of the current educational reforms, it will be worth looking at A-level and the rationale that perpetuates it, since it constitutes, still, in the minds of many able pupils, their parents, teachers and potential employers, the ultimate target of school education. As such it will act as a powerful force on the way reforms are viewed and its influence will permeate downwards into their implementation, acting, at the same time, through its mere existence, as a powerful disincentive to the majority of pupils.

The extent to which the Japanese succeed without such a system has been considered in Chapter 2. It might be argued that a strong cultural difference is the predisposing factor in the acceptance of general education in Japan. However, if we make comparisons nearer to home, we can perceive very important differences in our general education standard and that of France. About 375,000–400,000 students flow annually into the *'Bac'* (*Ministère de l'Education Nationale* figures 1984) compared with an A-level entry of about 250,000 in Britain (estimated by White 1988). Thus half as many again in France, with only a marginally higher population, are educated to 18-plus. Furthermore, the French qualification, spanning six or seven subjects, is obtained by more than 66 per cent. In Britain only half of the A-level entry from schools obtains three passes and in FE colleges the average pass rate is just over one subject (White 1988).

It is worth putting A-level into some sort of perspective. In terms of content, difficulty and specialization a three A-levels course has been compared to an American first degree. The student aspires to a very high level of competence in three subjects. On the other hand, education outside the specialist area is almost entirely lacking. For instance, only a small minority do A-level mathematics, the rest, generally, do none. The same is true of English, sciences, and foreign languages. We do a disservice to even our brightest pupils by giving them an education limited in breadth. Subject for subject, A-level is more demanding than the *'Bac'* but the gain in high academic standards has to be set against the wastage that the A-level 'gate' imposes by excluding large numbers who would have benefited themselves and the nation's economic progress through continued education.

Leaving aside for the moment the demotivating effect that A-level has on the bulk of children, it is not especially congruent with the needs of the nation in relation to the brightest products of the schools. There are growing needs, in the modern world, for transferability of skills, a broad compass of education and a willingness for people to move, during their working lifetimes, out of specialist subject areas. The call for engineers into management is a good example. If we are to compete with Japan, and to cope with the Japanization of our own industries, the high flexibility that derives from sound general education is an indispensable pre-condition.

Britain currently has a nationwide shortage of competent mathematicians – the only pool available to us is that tiny fraction of the school population that go on to do A-level mathematics. Not the least part of this problem is the current shortage of maths teachers. The narrow gate of specialization is in danger of running us out of the human resources needed to perpetuate the system. Britain produced only 9,665 mathematics graduates in 1986 from both universities and polytechnics and of these only 516 entered the teaching profession. Projections for 1995 show a shortfall in the numbers of mathematics teachers of between 4,000 and 12,000 (Smithers and Robinson 1988). Much of the teaching of mathematics is presently done by non-specialists many of whom, themselves, have not been educated beyond O-level standard in the subject. Without a broad education to 18-plus that includes continued mathematics, as well as other subjects defined as important in the national curriculum, and that encompasses much more of the population, it is doubtful if our resource problem can be solved. Such a solution would be needed as a precursor to wider entry into higher education.

As a guide to the likely outcome at degree level it is now generally recognized that A-level is not a particularly good indicator. In addition, changes in the nature of A-level courses seem to be out of step with those in the rest of education:

> It is very difficult to find any continuity and progression post-16 now O-levels have disappeared. A-levels in isolation are increasingly an anachronism between compulsory education and an increasingly flexible higher education system, neither continuing to develop the skills obtained in GCSE nor developing the skills needed for higher education.
>
> (Prof. D. West to ASE conference in TES 13.1.1989)

A-level is too difficult for the majority of pupils and there is still little else on offer. Those of average ability leave school with an education insufficient to meet the challenges of the modern world because the existence of A-level has been a major promoter of the belief, widely and realistically held, that post-compulsory education is for an academically inclined elite.

Because schools feel that they must be seen to succeed within the present ground rules, the deleterious effects of A-level courses are not confined to years 6 and 7. They spill over into the curriculum and organization of the years of compulsory secondary schooling. The content of teaching material up to 16-plus, the arrangement of subject options available to pupils in the fourth and fifth years and the segregation into ability sets, where these exist, must bear in mind the requirements of entry into A-level for the minority who are capable of doing so. This produces a distorting effect on the material taught to younger pupils of medium or lower ability or involves their separation from the brighter pupils from whom they might otherwise learn.

The foreword to the Higginson report summarized the views of many who gave evidence to the committee in a passage written by one of them.

> The most fundamental error in the traditional GCE/A-level system was that each stage was designed to be suited to those who were going on to the next. Schoolchildren who were not good enough to go on were regarded as expendable. The other view, that seems to be held in every other advanced country, is that each stage of education should be designed for the main body of those who take it and the following stage has to start from where the previous stage ended.
>
> (DES April 1988)

An example of the way in which the thinking of the education service, personified in some of its teachers, has fossilized around the all-consuming requirements of A-level, was evident at a recent conference in Wales. An extremely thoughtful and articulate HMI was explaining the new philosophy of the government's policy statement 'Science 5 to 16'. He quite rightly, in my view, stated that the intention of the policy was to improve the overall scientific literacy of the population and that the trend of the new policy would be towards balanced science courses rather than separate physics, chemistry and biology. At this point he paused, knowing the instinctive response that would come from his audience of science teachers, 'What about pupils who will wish to go on to take physics, chemistry and biology at A-level?' The HMI pointed out patiently that only a small fraction of the school population of 16-year olds stayed on to do *any science subjects* and of these the proportion wanting this combination in particular was very small indeed. Was it reasonable, therefore, to constrain the general good of the younger school population by teaching courses aimed at providing a ground work for future courses for the very few, he went on to ask. Would it not be better to rethink the contents of the A-level courses? To this I would add – would it not be better to rethink *the existence of the A-level courses*?

Angela Rumbold, the Education Minister, said that A-level would be abolished over her dead body. Clear thinking on the purposes of education is not assisted by gut reactions of this kind. It is a simple appeal to the hearts of those who, along with their children, are the principal beneficiaries of a system that actively denies opportunity to the majority. Sad prospect though it may be, the image of Mrs Rumbold lying moribund in the wake of progress should be no deterrent to the abolition of A-level.

If we are to learn from the Japanese example, the achievement of higher staying-on rates could be assisted by providing, in years 6 and 7, general courses that continue the work of the years up to the end of compulsory schooling. This, of course, would imply that the universities would have to teach all their own material rather than having a substantial portion of it taught by schools in A-level courses. It is a common experience, of science teachers in particular, that they are now teaching, at A-level, topics they themselves did not study until undergraduate level. The tendency to push increasing amounts of what is more properly degree material into the schools is a continuing trend that renders A-level even less accessible to the great majority of pupils.

In 1986 Professor Maurice Shock, the chairman of the Committee of Vice Chancellors of Universities, said they were considering the abolition of A-level and they were seeking an examination which would be taken by a wider range of pupils. A fundamental rethink was needed, in Professor Shock's opinion, of our whole approach to education beyond the compulsory level. He regarded the new, 'half-an-A-level' examination, called A/S, as being a totally inadequate contribution towards a broader curriculum. The depth of difficulty in A/S is no less than that of A-level; its content is simply less. The aim of the committee is to increase the number of pupils staying on beyond the age of 16 (*Observer* 12.10.86). As far as I am able to determine, this piece of seminal thinking has never been heard of again.

The report of the Higginson committee on A-level fared no better. It would not, in any case, in my view, have addressed the central problem of A-level's exclusivity through difficulty of the courses. Higginson was firm in the recommendation that present standards should not be relaxed. 'Candidates must continue to be drawn from a high-ability group. It is an indispensable feature of the A-level system that it maintain high standards' (DES April 1988).

Higginson was much more concerned with increasing the breadth of study at A-level, a worthy if insufficient objective, than increasing total access. The report was unceremoniously tossed out by the Conservative government which clearly supported the Rumbold line of intestinal thinking.

At the 1988 conference of the National Association of Headteachers, David Hart, General Secretary, called for the introduction of compulsory full- or part-time education to the age of 18 (TES 3.6.88). Voluntary staying on would be better, but, I imagine, like many in the profession, David Hart considers this unlikely to happen in sufficient numbers to make an impact on our urgent problem.

In the war years our continued education shortfall was dimly perceived and recognized in a never-implemented section of the 1944 Education Bill. A general duty was laid upon local authorities to establish and maintain county colleges for compulsory day-continuation attendance by young people (Barnett 1987).

A recent survey carried out by Professor Neville Postlethwaite of Hamburg University placed British pupils at the bottom of a league of 17 nations in science. Postlethwaite believes that the over-emphasis on high flyers could be to blame: 'Is it that this system of education is fostering high performance at the expense of mass education?' (Postlethwaite 1988).

Professor Sig Prais suggests that the Japanese system, where a large proportion of pupils stays on beyond school-leaving age, acts as a motivator for younger pupils to achieve well in their studies (Prais 1987). This motivation is lacking in British schools where there is a low staying-on rate. I would place much of the blame for this squarely on the shoulders of A-level. It is a major limiting factor in getting pupils to remain in school beyond the age of 16.

Well before compulsory education ends two different sub-cultures are likely to have developed in a school, consisting of the pupils who are determined to make something of their education and those who are not. The boundary between the two is roughly coterminous with that dividing the potential A-level students from the rest. There is a wide disparity of ethos between the two groups and, often, a degree of outright hostility. From the under achievers especially comes a type of defensive resentment towards, or a total incomprehension of, the motives of the achievers. One could hardly believe that the two sub-cultures exist within, and are products of, the same education system let alone the same school. Unfortunately, all too often, the division reproduces quite closely, in my experience, the class boundary between the middle and working class. 'The better pupils' come from 'the better areas'. For the weaker pupils, the absence of any real possibility of onward progression in school, beyond compulsory education, reinforces the difference. We urgently need a unified system where education to the age of 18 is an accepted norm and in which all pupils can participate to the best of their ability.

We need to ask ourselves what, apart from the entrenched attitudes in schools, might be responsible for the perpetuation of the A-level system. Again we are confronted with our own propensity to erect disincentives. Britain's universities, except for Oxford and Cambridge who are prepared to admit that they are better than the rest, maintain roughly equal standards. They set comparable entrance requirements relating almost entirely to A-level grades and award degrees that are nationally regarded as equivalent. Outside the universities the CNAA exists to ensure this equivalence. There is, in fact, some informal stratification, between the universities and between departments of some, which have gained a good reputation, and others less well regarded. The polytechnics are not held in the same esteem as the universities. However, in comparison with Japan, the stratification is slight, the number of places available few, and the entrance requirements, for degree courses at least, stringent enough to admit students drawn from only about the two top deciles of attainment.

Britain offers higher education to only about 14 per cent of each age cohort – the places available determine the grade requirements for entry. Mr Baker intended that this admission rate should rise to about 15 or 16 per cent by the 1990s and to 18 or 20 per cent by the end of the century. In Japan it is already about 36 per cent but Japan does not operate a system of equivalence in its universities. Japan's institutions of higher education are quite finely stratified, a parallel, as we shall see later, to the gradation of the upper secondary schools (see Chapter 4). Tokyo university stands at the pinnacle followed by a number of ranked public and private universities of high repute and succeeding layers of universities and colleges down to those of the lowest esteem. There are, however, in Japan, far more opportunities for acquiring higher education of some sort. The most able have the incentive of Tokyo, Kyoto, etc.; those of more modest ability can set their sights lower whilst retaining the incentive to study and achieve their best.

In essence, the difference is that Britain offers a small number of places with little real difference in standards or entrance requirements; Japan offers many more places with greater discrepancies in order to accommodate a much wider range of the population. John MacGregor or some future Secretary of State, will have to choose between these alternatives; it is not possible to have high admission and uniform standard set at the highest level. Mr Baker seemed, indeed, to be preparing the ground for change in his speech to the higher education conference Lancaster University: 'The structures appropriate to higher education with . . . 13 per cent participation, simply cannot be sustained when participation rises to 30 per cent' (TES 13.1.89). Mr Baker went on to talk about a much more diversified system like that in the United States. The system in the latter country is much more like the Japanese system than ours is.

Britain's demotivatingly small number of places available in higher education uses A-level as a convenient and easily operated gateway. It shuts out those of average abilities who might have benefited from some form of higher education had we been able to admit to anything other than stringent uniformity in higher-education qualifications.

WHERE CAN WE START THE REFORM OF A-LEVELS?

There seems little possibility, realistically, that A-level will be abolished outright in favour of a type of 'continued [higher] GCSE' operated as a national curriculum to age 18. However, economic circumstances may force some change. By the mid-1990s the population of 16- to 19-year olds will have fallen dramatically. There will simply not be enough A-level students around to provide for the various requirements of industry and other employments currently seeking this type of qualified school leaver. Higher education may be facing a severe drop in the numbers it can attract. We might, therefore, expect a little belated support from the universities and polytechnics in promoting a broader access to continued education.

The starting point may well have to be AS-level: 'As yet it is an imperfect instrument − but it is, after the disappointing rejection of Dr Higginson's report, the only instrument we've got. Schools need to be helped to use it' (Michael Duffy, TES 6.1.89).

At present AS is greatly underused. A large proportion of students simply take one AS to top up a traditional A-level course. Only 420 students, nationwide, were taking two AS and two A-levels (ibid.). In a situation of diminishing teacher resources, it is difficult to see how the extra demand that these courses would impose, can be met.

The Association for Science Education, ASE, has proposed three models for reform of 16−19 science, two of which, in fact, are more radical than the Higginson Report (TES, 13.1.89). The first would be directly equivalent to A and AS levels but would involve students in building a compulsory core in each subject. The second proposes a common (national curricular type?) core of science studies for all students and the third is entirely modular, allowing students to tailor their courses to suit their own purposes.

None of these measures alone, or ultimately, will be sufficient. What ASE proposes for science has equal applicability in all the national curricular subjects. Neither will the measures above increase access to continued education to those whose ability is not sufficient to tackle A-level or courses of a comparable standard.

However, what these proposals indicate is that a re-think is underway. We need to go a step at a time. We need to start from where we are now, not where we should like to be. Reform of post-compulsory education must go hand in hand with other measures in the pipeline:

[The GCSE] examination has been acclaimed as a success by the Secretary of State. . . . Surely there can be no stronger reason to change the existing A-level syllabuses and examinations making them consistent with GCSE and thus ensuring a similar improvement in standards at 18-plus.

(Secondary Heads' Association November 1988)

BRITAIN'S UNDER-ACHIEVERS

Apart from producing over-specialized 18-year olds, at the top of the ability range, and failing to produce a sufficiently educated and motivated middle range, the British education system is unsurpassed in the developed world, for releasing educational rejects at the bottom of the ability range. These pupils leave school without qualifications and often without the simple basic skills of numeracy and literacy. The failure to educate them sufficiently guarantees the perpetuation of a large, unthinking stratum of society, a segment of the population unable and unwilling to contribute to the well-being of the nation.

a *World In Action* investigation revealed that as many as seven million – nearly one in eight of the population – could have difficulties reading, writing and adding up. The programme's literacy and numeracy survey of 1,000 adults and teenagers in Rochdale showed an alarming number of people unable to read and understand a fire notice, unable to do simple multiplication and struggling to work out 50 per cent of 180. . . . It isn't that there are more illiterate people today, or that educational standards have fallen. We've always had the problem, but it's been exposed by unemployment.

(Listener 5.2.87)

Former Education Minister, Chris Patten, said, in 1986, that Britain was in danger of producing a 'yob society'. I take this to mean a society in which a significant proportion of the population is insufficiently educated, unable to comprehend the needs of society and its responsibilities to it, is a drain on the economy rather than a contributor to it and, when it becomes a sufficient proportion of the population, is self-perpetuating from one generation to the next.

A British visitor to Japan quickly becomes aware of a different ethos in the people around him from the one that prevails here. The people on the streets, in their homes, offices and shops seem more purposeful. The general quality of clothing, cleanliness, and grooming is better. The discrepancies between people are smaller and it is much more difficult to categorize by class and occupation. Japan has the lowest crime rate in the developed world and the fewest lawyers per head of population. Banks do not even have barriers between the cashiers and the customers. In the carriages of trains flimsy advertising posters are suspended from the ceilings and are not torn down. Unprotected automatic vending machines, containing, sometimes, hundreds of pounds worth of goods are common even in badly lit side streets. The streets are free from litter and the public telephones are not vandalized. For a short period I used to travel each day from the coastal city of Kamakura, by the Yokosuka line, into central Tokyo. Each morning, having arrived at Kamakura station, I would reserve my place in the queue for a train, by placing my camera on the ground whilst I went off to the station kiosk. I never failed to find both my camera and place intact on my return. It is common, even in shops selling very high-cost and eminently portable goods, for the shopkeeper to remain 'in the back' until called; the potential customer, or browser, is trusted not to steal things.

I remember vividly, once, my return to Britain and the shock I felt standing on the platform of Reading station. The huge and startling discrepancies in demeanour and the apparent, large differences in the quality of life were so obvious that I wondered why I had never really noticed them before. I felt compelled to take my luggage into the toilet with me to avoid the risk of theft. The toilet was filthy, vandalized and ridden with graffiti.

Britain has become a country with a low fund of common cultural capital. By this I mean that the shared experiences in work, in educational background, in outlook and knowledge are too small for us to maintain or regenerate a national ethos towards the improvement of our society in the same degree that other developed nations are able to do. My definition of 'common cultural capital' has nothing to do with racial background or religious outlook. It is about the degree of transactional knowledge, held by each member of society, sufficient to allow understanding to take place between people and about the concerns of the society. In that sense it transcends racial issues within a society such as Britain's. Ideally, in an educated world, it would span national boundaries.

Within its own society the Japanese education system goes much further than ours towards guaranteeing, irrespective of academic ability, a large fund of shared cultural capital amongst the members of its society. If one were confronted with a randomly selected 18-year old in Japan one could predict with considerable accuracy what educational experience he had been exposed to, what he would be likely to know to some degree and the general tenor of his moral attitudes and outlook on society. It is unlikely that this would be the case in Britain. If two young persons, even if they had attended the same school, were chosen, it would be difficult to guarantee any real community of educational experience between them, other than in the most simplistic parameters of school life.

One of the ways to ensure a greater community of educational experience is through a national curriculum. This is discussed in detail in Chapter 5. Another way is to ensure that a full benefit, for every child, is had from the education service. This is not currently the case.

Interviews with German school children, in the television programme *Educating Britain* revealed the constant reiteration of phrases like 'I need', 'I must pass', 'although I am not good at and do not like [maths] I must work hard at it'. The pupils were referring to the school leavers' examination which is essential if they are to go on to training or further education. Children in Rochdale were interviewed in a cafe where they were truanting. Any sense of educational urgency was missing from their remarks. They were, in my experience of a large number of schools, typical of a substantial segment of British school children – perhaps 30 or 40 per cent of the total in some areas of the country.

Much of the underachievement in British schools stems from the poor attitudes of pupils (and in many cases their parents), from indiscipline and classroom disruption and from truancy. There is very little, if anything, in the 1988 Education Reform Act that would confront these issues. It is unlikely, for example, that anything in the 'competition-directed' legislation will have any bearing on such problems. It is equally unlikely that 'parent power' will produce the results. As often as not, in the case of truants and disruptors, the most difficult task for the school is to elicit the interest and co-operation of the parents. So frequently that it becomes depressing, I have heard colleagues bemoan the fact that they are often confronted by a challenge on discipline from the parent. Or, on the other hand, they have encountered no more than a supine acceptance, by the parent, that schooling is a legal requirement that is to be resented and borne or an admission that the parent can give little help. Mr Baker's legislation takes an optimistic view of the participation of such parents in the education process. Perhaps this is simply not the type of parent Mr Baker is interested in or knows much about.

Yet for improved performance of the education process, most teachers would regard these as the priority areas. In my own view, if these problems were solved, more good would be done to the system than by the agency of any other change. Table 3.3 indicates the scale of the problem.

BRITAIN'S LACK OF EDUCATIONAL DETERMINATION

The education law states that children shall attend school until the age of 16. It does not, however, insist that they learn anything. The system does not demand any minimum standard of achievement. The law does not even insist that a child *attempt to achieve* a minimum standard. Truancy is illegal but the law is invoked in only a small number of cases relative to the size of the truancy problem. Disruption in schools is a problem that grows yearly. It can be so bad in some classes, or even in whole schools, that effective education comes to a halt. What has been the response to this? In typical British fashion we have consistently and perversely walked away from the solution that the core

Table 3.3 Secondary teachers physically assaulted or threatened in last year (A) and verbally abused in last year (B) and serious interruptions to teaching (C), (228 teachers)

A		B		C	
Response	%	*Response*	%	*Response*	%
No	94	No	66	Yes	44
Yes (by pupil)	4	Yes (by pupil)	11	No	56
Yes (by parent)	1	Yes (by parent)	13		

Source: Adapted from *Teacher* 13.6.88

of each problem implies. At best there has been a nibbling away at the fringes; at worst we have engaged in some displacement activity that has no direct bearing on the problem at all. Government and local authorities have failed totally to prioritize their targets for improvement. Massive and costly initiatives like the introduction of GCSE may or may not improve the educational standard of the whole population. Only the future will reveal whether the effort has been worthwhile or not. What is absolutely sure is that it will have nothing like the same beneficial effects that would be obtained by setting a minimum standard that all pupils must achieve, ensuring that all pupils attend school full-time and that all classes are sufficiently well behaved for teaching to go on.

Ironically, the changes that would do the greatest good would be much cheaper than the marginal and unfocused attempts that are made at present. Some would actually have a cost benefit to the education service. They would, however, require determination to put them into effect. They have the advantage, however, that they would be simple to operate and easy to communicate to the population – two attributes spectacularly missing from enterprises like GCSE and the 1988 ERA.

In order to meet the presumed intention of compulsory education, that is, that pupils learn something, it would be necessary to set a minimum standard of education for school leavers. Instead of qualifying to leave school on an age basis alone, an age plus attainment basis could be set. The attainment target range for each key stage of education under the national curriculum could well serve such a purpose. The national curriculum documentation is curiously silent on what happens when the target range is not achieved. Nor are there any suggestions about how the education service will respond to those, especially

14- and 16-year olds, whose comment on the attainment tests will simply be to absent themselves. Sir Rhodes Boyson feels that pupils who did not achieve this standard within the normal span of schooling would need an extra compulsory period in school (*Teachers' Weekly* 1988). Below is suggested a way in which extra compulsory education might easily be promoted. This would act as a sharp incentive for pupils to reach the required standard. To avoid any unfair discrimination against children with genuine learning difficulties or handicaps, an allowance could be made. There is already a mechanism for identifying the most seriously disadvantaged children in the process of 'statementing' for special educational provision.

Truants are breaking the law of the land. Without any further changes, the enforcement of the law could be tightened up. This would, I agree, impose a considerable burden on the courts. However, the spirit, if not the letter of the law is, that a child shall have completed a certain number of years of schooling before being entitled to leave school. Much better would be to make changes that promoted the compulsory nature of education. A simple change in the law to make sure that any periods of truancy were automatically added on, at the end of compulsory schooling, would rapidly reduce the rate of truancy. Until the extra period had been completed young people would not be eligible for work, training schemes or unemployment benefit. They would be explicitly unable to obtain income until the time had been made up. Such a change in the law would not only have a salutory effect on children but on the large number of parents who currently condone, or conspire in, their children's truancy.

The third problem, disruption of classes, not only affects the standard of education of those who engage in it, but destroys the chances of those who genuinely want to make progress with their education. It is also likely to have a deeply corrosive effect on society. Many ex-disrupters grow up to have as scant a regard for the law as they had for the authority of the school. Corporal punishment in schools is now, thankfully, at an end. Apart from doing little to cure the problems of disruption, it was a dehumanizing device that a modern society should not, I feel, use as a model of authority for young people. Instead, a framework in which pupils are constrained to use self-discipline, or suffer the consequences (that is the general principle of law), should be employed. If a pupil, by his or her behaviour, puts the education of other pupils at risk, that pupil must face the probability of exclusion from school for a period of time. Provision for this is made under the 1986 Education Act but what is lacking is follow-up which would constrain the disruptor to view his attitude as contrary to his own interest. Many disruptors regard a period of exclusion as a reward rather than a punishment; behaviour, on return to school, is unaffected or worsened. The same device as I proposed for truants could apply. Time during which the exclusion had been operative would be added on and the pupil would have delayed, by his own folly, the day when he could officially leave school and receive income.

Headteachers might be reluctant to carry the burden of decision about whether a pupil should be delayed access to income because of exclusion. Fortunately, under the 1986 Act there are quite specific clauses on exclusion that involve school governors and the LEA as well as the headteacher. There is also an appeal structure. With little modification this structure could be used to administer the exclusion and 'added time before availability for income' structure I am proposing.

Most LEAs have some kind of final recourse for severe disruptors. The last stop is often residential care of some kind. This is immensely expensive. Candidates for this provision will often enter an out-of-county establishment. The cost to the education authority will be about £14,000–£18,000 per child per year. Three such pupils will therefore have more spent on them in a year, £42,000–£54,000, than the entire capitation for a medium to large comprehensive school. The capitation is used to buy books, stationery, equipment and so on. It seems less than sensible to continue throwing money after pupils who have put themselves beyond the pale of normal education by their behaviour. The extra money would go a long way to helping the majority of pupils to achieve as many of them deserve and wish to do.

Many might regard my remarks in the preceding paragraphs as draconian measures to achieve minimum attainment and to improve attendance and behaviour in schools. German, Japanese, and French school children do not seem to need these strictures. I believe there are two reasons why we need to act with more determination than others find necessary. By a concentration on the education of elites we have failed to interest a very large segment of the population in the process of education – it has become devalued in our society. The under-achievers, truants and disruptors of today will become the parents of tomorrow's pupils. We must break that cycle decisively. The second reason is that, in Britain, we have made the effects of failed education inconsequential, in the short term, in the perceptions of many individual pupils and their parents. The too-ready availability of state safety nets in the form of benefit payments, unqualified entry into schemes like YTS and the historical existence of many employment opportunities that demand nothing in terms of education or proper training, have jointly conspired to promote the inconsequential nature of education in the minds of the non-aspiring, the irresponsible and those who can only think short term. The combination of these two reasons has been devastating to the education system, the economy and the nature of our society.

ADEQUATE MANPOWER USAGE

Teachers are employed by the local authority and could, legitimately, be located in any of the authority's schools, or, be moved from school to school as the authority saw fit. Until falling rolls hit the schools the redeployment of teachers was virtually unknown. In the present falling-rolls situation a minimum of redeployment is used to remove overstaffing in particular schools to fill vacancies in others. However, the use of LEA-directed redeployment in order to balance out the strengths and weaknesses in its various schools is almost unheard of. Most authorities seem happy to contemplate, for example, a situation in which the physics department in one school may be in crisis because of a high proportion of poor or underqualified teachers, whilst the school down the road thrives in physics because of superabundance of high-quality staff.

The type of managerial balancing act needed to produce adequacy in both schools is seldom attempted. The solution to the problem is left with the headteacher without, however, giving them the powers of hiring and firing that they would need to do the job effectively. Indeed, for long periods of time, the authority may be 'officially' unaware of the situation. Only when under-performance by a member of staff, or a whole department, becomes chronic and an issue of public outcry, does the authority normally intervene. Any solution it may then propose is unlikely to involve constructive redeployment of staff from a better-endowed school.

Setting aside the general inertia of LEAs in respect of detailed manpower planning, there is one reason why this solution is unfavourable. There is direct accountability through local elections. The governing body, of the school that might lose one or more of its good physicists, is likely to contain a few county and district councillors. They do not want to be seen as the people who connived at making their local school worse even if, in so doing, one in a neighbouring district was improved. Parochialism inhibits planned solutions.

The 1988 Education Act will make rotation of teachers even more difficult by weakening LEA control. The specific provisions connected with the local management of schools will make of each school an island unto itself. The school is expected to use its relatively miniscule power, within the education system (market?) as a whole, to secure the staff it needs. Yet its power to trade off, shed, buy in or dismiss staff except in extreme circumstances, will be very limited.

Prefectural education authorities in Japan rotate teachers on a regular basis. The transition from one school to another is much easier than it is in this country because of the national curriculum that operates. This rotation ensures a much more even spread of expertise through the schools of the prefecture than is possible at present within a British LEA. The irony of the present situation is that, because of the damping effect the Japanese national curriculum has on differences that could arise from variation in teacher competence, Japanese prefectures probably need teacher rotation less than we presently do. If we allow different interpretations of the syllabuses we need frequent rotation so that the methods known to one school are transmitted to others.

Teacher rotation, if it is to be effective, implies teacher appraisal. The dispute, that took place in British education during 1986 and 1987, had the resistance to teacher assessment as one of its central issues and is probably symptomatic of a general resistance in the education service to being managed. The managerial 'amateur status' of many heads is a further manifestation of the same resistance. The headteachers within each prefecture in Japan are not only rotated around the schools but also spend periods of time working in the prefectural administration of education. This must have a leavening effect in two directions. It introduces, into the prefectural machinery, experience of what schools are actually like and the realities of the problems they face, and it also widens the experience of heads, in management terms, and in the understanding of the complexities of the bureaucracy that runs the education service. Needless to say, no such systematization of manpower usage occurs in the British education system.

Because systematic rotation of teachers does not take place within British LEAs, teachers are able to spend substantially all their careers in the same school if they feel so inclined, and many do. Consequently, a school can develop an idiosyncratic character. The degree of idiosyncrasy is aggravated by permeability to innovations of which the school will, over time, have made its own particular selection. Staff, who remain in one school for a very long period of time, may come to regard their own school's particular way of doing things as the right way or the only way. They may suffer from a reduced standard of expectations about the generality of education.

This situation does not predispose teachers in affluent areas to appreciate the social problems of education in poorer areas nor to seek some equalization of the educational provision across the nation. In the deprived areas a static teaching force may settle, jellied in contentment, for second best, unaware that it could do better.

4

Examinations and progression
through the system

In attempting an assessment of GCSE, and the impact it is likely to make on the educational standard of the nation, and the degree to which it might increase our competitiveness, we need to ask several questions.

- What are its aims? Will they be achieved?
- Will it sufficiently raise the educational standard of the whole nation to make us competitive with countries like Japan?
- Will it act as an incentive to the development of a 'learning culture'?

It must be said at the outset that GCSE is in its infancy and judgements at this stage may be premature. I shall try to consider the potential of GCSE in the light of what progress seems feasible and ask whether or not such progress will be sufficient and in the right direction. It will be fair to speculate on what has been left out of the GCSE package. Following the questions about GCSE I shall consider the Japanese examination system.

WHAT ARE THE AIMS OF GCSE? WILL THEY BE ACHIEVED?

A full statement of aims is available in government publications. The following, however, reduces them to the practical terms in which they have been interpreted at school level.

1   *There is to be a much wider admission of pupils into the examination system without a lowering of standards.*

As a rule of thumb the government expects that 80 to 90 per cent of pupils passing through the system will reach the same standard in examination as the notional 60 per cent achieved formerly under O-level and CSE.

This objective can, of course, only be realized if the teaching and learning processes in schools improve. Simply manipulating the award of grades to accommodate the extra 20 to 30 per cent of pupils would be to engage in national self-delusion on a grand scale. A bold step has been taken in GCSE in attempting to incorporate elements of the examination into aspects of the teaching process. Thus, course work, done by pupils in school, or practical work in science and technological subjects, are assessed for examination purposes. This clearly holds some potential for raising standards. The course work, because it comprises a part of the examination, is likely to have a higher incentive value for pupils than might otherwise be the case.

At the time of writing this section, the first set of GCSE results had just been published. I believe there exists within the teaching profession a cautious optimism that GCSE has had some motivating effect and that there has been some raising of standards. At this stage, the first of these, estimating improvement in motivation, can be no more than a subjective interpretation by one observer from informal conversation with colleagues around the country and acknowledgement to HMI who reported, 'positive effects on teaching and learning in secondary schools' (HMI Interim report March 1988).

The case for improvement in standards must rest on the interpretation of nationwide figures showing the distribution of candidates through the seven grades A to G. The subjects shown in Table 4.1 are chosen from amongst the ones which will form core and foundation subjects in the national curriculum (see Chapter 5). The first notable feature is the wide disparity between subjects, in the percentages of candidates obtaining the various grades. Clearly some subjects are taken by highly selected candidates. French and German, in which the proportions gaining A grades is high, would be an example of this – in many schools these are subjects taken only by more able candidates. (In Greek, hardly a subject for the mainstream of education, 62.6 per cent of the 1,276 candidates gained A grades, an extreme example of the point I am making).

Table 4.1 Grades awarded in GCSE in selected subjects, summer 1988

Subject	No. 1,000s	A	B	C	% Candidates in each grade Cum A + B + C	D	E	F	G
English	654.7	6.6	14.2	22.8	43.6	23.2	17.9	10.3	4.0
Maths	661.6	6.2	8.9	21.7	36.8	16.4	16.3	15.4	7.1
Biology	293.9	7.3	12.4	23.1	36.8	19.2	14.4	12.2	8.5
Chemistry	214.8	10.6	14.7	23.0	48.3	18.7	14.0	10.6	5.2
Physics	245.2	9.1	14.5	21.1	48.7	19.7	16.9	12.0	5.8
French	238.1	19.9	14.6	15.6	50.1	17.9	14.4	11.6	4.7
German	68.7	20.7	15.3	16.7	52.7	17.5	13.6	10.9	4.4
Geography	295.1	7.8	14.0	19.5	41.3	19.1	16.4	12.5	7.3
History	242.8	9.8	15.0	19.3	44.1	17.4	15.5	11.9	7.6
CDT	157.0	6.8	11.4	16.9	35.1	19.0	18.8	15.4	7.6
Home Econ	187.5	4.1	10.0	19.1	33.2	21.2	20.0	15.1	7.3

Source: Adapted from TES 2.9.88

In Maths and English, subjects taken by the vast majority of pupils, the award of A grades is much more modest. CDT and Home Economics – subjects which have suffered unjustifiably from discrimination by school curriculum managers, parents and pupils and have attracted an undue proportion of less able candidates – show the lowest percentages of A, B, and C grades.

There is little doubt that the overall percentage of pupils gaining A, B, and C grades, in GCSE, is higher than it was under the old system. The top three grades in GCSE are intended to equate in standards to O-level grades A to C. Dennis Hatfield, chairman of the joint council for GCSE, said that not only had standards been maintained but more pupils had slightly better grades (TES 2.9.88).. The questions remaining are:

(a) Can the two exams, GCSE and the former system, be equated?

(b) What validity can be placed on the results – have standards risen or was the exam easier or marked more leniently?

(a) In equating the two systems one must put one's faith in the experience of examiners who were charged with the responsibility for carrying over the standards of previous years into the new exam. This, however, is not a simple task. The complicating element of large course-work components is one for which, in many subjects, there existed no previous standard against which a judgement could be made. The extreme complexity of the way GCSE exam papers are constructed to achieve differentiation (see below) was another factor which may reduce the validity of comparison.

(b)   The second problem, at present, is that in allocating the candidates to grades, the uncomfortable mixture of norm and criterion referencing used in the former examinations was maintained. In pure norm referencing the shape of the outcome is a self-fulfilling prophecy. Whatever the overall standard, a fixed percentage of candidates, will be allocated to each grade. This is demotivating for the weaker candidate; he cannot set his sights on the achievement of a particular set of objectives or known criteria that will result in a particular grade. His reward is constrained by how well, or badly, other candidates perform. In pure criterion referencing, certain fixed expectations are set for each grade and a candidate who meets these criteria gets the grade irrespective of how well or badly other candidates do in the same exam. In this country we have always operated both systems to some extent in all subject examinations (Mobley *et al.* 1986).

At this stage it is very difficult to gauge the degree to which the mix of norm and criterion referencing under the new and old systems remained the same. My own guess is that it was substantially different but without very detailed statistical data from the boards it is not possible to make definitive statements.

It was perhaps unfortunate that some anonymous examiners announced that the percentage of pupils to be awarded each grade in the various subjects had been set in advance of the papers being marked – i.e. they were norm referenced ahead of time – with the implication that this enabled the results to be massaged upwards. This contribution to the debate would have been more valuable had they identified themselves and explained their evidence.

A hopeful sign, for the future of GCSE grading, is that an attempt is being made to set grade-related criteria for certain grades. Knowing exactly what achievement would give a particular result would go a long way towards the clarification of the teaching and the motivation of pupils.

The setting of grade-related criteria is, however, producing many problems. Not least of these relate to the extreme complexity of the way the examinations are set. An aim of GCSE is to test a wide range of cognitive, and, in many subjects, practical skills in an attempt to get away from an over-reliance on factual recall. Compounded by the requirements of differentiation, comparability across different subjects, and the variability in course-work requirements, the erection of grade-related criteria is proving to be a very difficult and contentious task. We are forced to wonder if the examination has been made too complex and if it is trying to achieve too much. In a seminar for head-teachers, a few months prior to the launch of GCSE, a chief examinations officer for one of the boards reported on the results of some of the pilot studies. Having gone through the complexities of assessment in the GCSE mode, his team had found that the allocation of candidates to grades almost exactly replicated that made when the same candidates were assessed on simple factual recall tests. If this is true generally, GCSE will have proved expensive, time-consuming and unnecessary. It will be a prime example of the tendency in British education to substitute intentions for outcomes.

We shall see later that Japanese examinations tend to be much more straightforward, easy to assess and hence reliable in the sense they are internally valid. They may be open to the charge that they test predominantly the recall of authorized fact and lead to a didactical form of teaching but they do give clear and unambiguous results within the terms of their own objectives. In the Japanese system it is much more possible for both pupil and teacher to know what has to be achieved to reach a specific goal. The examination system works hand in glove, in this respect, with high specificity of the national curriculum.

The first objective, raising general standards, is also approached indirectly through the second objective of GCSE.

2 *Pupils are to be tested on 'what they know and can do' rather than the opposite.*
The rationale for this principle is that, in the past, we may have underestimated the capacities of youngsters by setting tests that were more designed to reveal what they did not know and could not do. It is a common experience of teachers that weak pupils spend much of their examination time doing nothing. They had been asked the wrong questions. Had the questions been designed differently, the candidates might have been productively

occupied showing that, at some level at least, there were skills and knowledge they could demonstrate. The achievement of this objective entrains the principle of 'differentiation', attempted through different devices in different subjects but essentially aiming to give the pupil both a teaching course and a level of examination that permits the candidate to demonstrate his full potential whatever that might be. It is fair to say that differentiation can never be perfect. Indeed, if one could precisely predict what level of examination a pupil could do well in, the examination itself would be superfluous. One marked danger of differentiation is that a pupil unprepared to put in sufficient effort might be content to take an easier paper, in subjects where multiple papers are the differentiating device. It is possible that differentiation could legitimize low expectations and underachievement.

The aim is laudable if it provides the incentive for a pupil to stretch himself. On the whole, in my limited experience of the two years GCSE has been in operation, there has been some beneficial effect in respect of aims 1 and 2. There seem to be, however, several factors that constrain what potential of the new examination can be developed in this direction.

The new examination will allocate candidates to the seven grades A to G depending on performance. A bad mistake was made in publicizing the fact that grades A to C would equate with the old O-level 'pass' grades A to C and the old CSE grade 1. The currency of the new examination will depend to a substantial extent on how results are regarded by employers. It will be very easy for the employer who has no great interest in the education system, to stick to his old requirements, e.g. four O-level passes, without making much attempt to understand, or value, the grading system of the new examination. It is a common experience of careers teachers and careers officers that many employers had not understood, nor placed any value upon, CSE despite the many years of its existence. How much more are we expecting if we hope they will review their recruiting practices to take account of the new examination?

Alarming evidence of employer ignorance of GCSE has come to light recently. A survey of 505 firms in January 1988, on behalf of the DES showed that only 35 per cent were able to say, without prompting, what GCSE was. A survey of 215 directors by the Institute of Directors showed that 193 out of 215 had heard of GCSE but only 35 said they could understand it (TES 2.9.88).

These are not surprising figures – they simply reflect the historically weak link between the education and employment systems in
Britain. Without strong employer recognition, the capacity of
the exam to act as an incentive for pupils intending to leave
school at 16-plus is severely curtailed.

A second factor which limits the power of GCSE to motivate
is, that for many of the middle- and lower-ability pupils, the
very ones that the British education system has failed for so
long, the examination is not a gateway to furtherance of their
education, it is merely a final judgement of it (see Chapter 3).
This factor, in combination with low regard accorded by
employers, and the two factors mutually reinforcing one
another, puts serious limitation on the ways in which any form of
16-plus final examination can be presented as a pupil motivator.
We shall see later in this chapter that the nearest equivalent
Japanese examinations are much more easily recognized as
grading 'gateways' rather than simply as gradings.

3   *GCSE aims to produce a greater degree of national uniformity and comparability in the different areas of the country.*
GCSE replaced the existing O-level and CSE boards with a
smaller number of GCSE boards and scrapped the existing and
incredible number of 19,000, different examination syllabuses.
Comparability across different boards is being attempted
through the devices of 'the national criteria', to which all
subjects must conform, and, in many individual subjects, the
'national subject-specific criteria'. The Secondary Examinations
Council (SEC) was charged with vetting submissions from the
boards before a syllabus and examination could be used for
GCSE.

This must be a step in the right direction. It conforms with the
principles behind the creation of a national curriculum and the
proposed 'benchmark' testing at 7, 11, 14, and 16. One is forced
to wonder, however, given that the SEC had great powers over
what the GCSE boards could do, why the SEC itself did not
become the sole examining board for the whole nation: 'If the
[examining] groups cannot agree to common practices and
format . . . then we would anticipate considerable pressure from
centres [schools etc.] for the establishment of a single examining
board' (*Teachers' Weekly* 5.9.88).

Right up to, and in some cases after the launch of GCSE
teaching in September 1986, almost all the boards were still

attempting to get certain subject syllabuses approved. Teaching began in these cases on the basis of the most educated guess teachers could make about what would be contained in the final approval. A great deal of time and expense was involved in sending submissions backwards and forwards between the boards and the SEC.

4   *Skills are to receive greater emphasis versus syllabus content than had formerly been the case under the old system.*
In general I am inclined to believe this a good move. Decisions about content, since only a very small fraction of what is available can be included in a syllabus, must be arbitrary. The motivating intention behind the greater emphasis placed on skills is that they are more universal and timeless than content, they develop the potential of people and have a greater transferability in employment and society.

There is a parallelism in this intention with the actuality in Japan. Japanese companies recruit for potential because they are specifically interested in flexibility and adaptability at all levels of the workforce. The way they do this, however, is by a recruitment process that is heavily dependent on formal academic qualifications acquired in a preponderantly content-dominated examination system. For example, top companies take, as first preference, those from the most prestigious of the hierarchically ranked universities. This method must be open to question from the British viewpoint. Admission to universities, in Japan, is the last step in a series of examinations which we would question as measures of potential. However, it can hardly be denied that, in the real world of outcomes, as opposed to the make-believe world of intentions, the Japanese system seems to work; the prestige companies that recruit the 'best' students are eminently successful and the identifying characteristics of their employees are transferability and flexibility in both skills and knowledge.

If the British system is going to sacrifice some of its content base in favour of skills it must be very sure of two things: that the desired skills can be better taught by a skills-based approach, and that, conversely, the skills would not as easily be acquired as a by-product of the content approach. Some of the more extreme advocates of the skills approach would have the content acquisition as the by-product. At present GCSE seems to have an acceptable content/skills balance.

One further caveat must be advanced against pushing the skills approach too far. Skills cannot be taught in vacuo; content must be a vehicle through which skills are acquired. If the choice of 'vehicular content' is left too much in the hands of examination boards, LEAs, headteachers and heads of subject departments, we are in some danger of reducing our capacity to create a common cultural capital of transactional knowledge in our society. The argument around this issue, at present, burns most brightly amongst historians. The skill of 'empathy' is hotly disputed. Proponents argue that the skills of the historian are more important than the acquisition of historical fact. In other words, to teach the skill of empathy, any piece of suitable content is as good as any other. Others argue that a sound and chronological appreciation of our history is a vital cultural asset and that skills like empathy should take a lesser part. Strong figures in the Conservative Party appear to fall into the latter camp. One assumes the compromise will be found in the construction of the national curriculum.

● *Will GCSE sufficiently raise the educational standard of the whole nation to enable us to compete with countries like Japan?* If GCSE is taken in isolation, the answer to this must be an emphatic 'no'. There is little in GCSE, that is immediately obvious, that would increase the staying-on rate beyond compulsory schooling, for example. At the inception of GCSE the opportunity was missed to question the whole idea of terminating education at 16-plus.

GCSE may have effects, at the margin, in raising whole nation standards up to 16-plus but, as we saw from the surveys of Japanese educational achievements, marginal effects will not be sufficient to make us competitive with the Japanese. In mathematics, for example, the attainments of our average 16-year olds are matched by average Japanese 13-year olds. Whatever else has been claimed for GCSE, no one has suggested that it will correct deficits of this magnitude.

One could take a less demanding view of the qualifier 'sufficiently'. Will GCSE sufficiently raise the standard of school leavers to make them more competent citizens? Will it make the training of 16-plus school leavers a more productive exercise? The shift of emphasis in the direction of transferable cognitive and practical skills, and especially those of problem solving might help in both cases. However, the question about training begs a question unrelated, directly, to GCSE. Improvements in training depend more than anything else on a change of heart in British industry. There does seem to be a growing awareness that industry, and government, could do more. Perhaps there is some hope that improvements made by GCSE will be capitalized upon.

Has GCSE the potential to evolve into an examination that will incrementally help to stimulate improvement? This is perhaps the fairest question one could ask about the 'sufficiency' of GCSE. The infant examination must be given a fair chance to develop its full form. Can it raise standards year by year? It is not easy to see this happening if it retains large elements of norm referencing – the standard in this case would be determined not by attainment criteria but by the attainment distribution of candidates. If grade-related criteria can be set, and gradually advanced at a pace that can be accommodated by the teaching and learning process, then the standard of attainment could be inched forward. It would require a conscious policy to do this and would need to recruit the co-operation of the teaching profession to attain known and agreed targets. This sounds terribly difficult to British ears; we are not good at national goal setting. However, in the early decades of the post-war era the Japanese nation made such a request of the education service in relation to mathematics. We have seen that a very high standard was achieved.

● *Will GCSE act as an incentive to the development of a 'learning culture?'*
The future will be one of ever-increasing pace of change. The access to education has increased rapidly over the last century, along with the shift towards egalitarianism that has characterized all the advanced nations. Change, and the increasing reliance on measured competence – 'experts' – will make it ever more necessary for people to hold qualifications and constantly to uprate them or acquire new ones if the old ones become obsolete. When we examine the redundancy of craft skills in the Midlands, for example, we see the need for the acquisition of new ones. In the teaching profession the once highly regarded classicists are now an unwanted breed. A nation's response to the future must be to stimulate the development of a learning culture. When we look at training in Japan we shall see this type of culture much more fully developed than it is at present in Britain (Chapter 8).

GCSE can do no more, I suspect, than co-operate with the exigencies, opportunities and stark realities that the future will impose. It is impossible, at this early stage, to make a judgement of its capacity to do this. Perhaps the most hopeful sign is simply that GCSE has come into existence. That fact alone suggests that Britain is capable of instituting sweeping reform on a nationwide scale. Five or ten years ago this would have been hardly believable. If GCSE contains the potential to evolve then it will play its part alongside the many other inputs that will create a 'learning culture'. The degree to which it acts as incentive will depend upon its capacity to stimulate education beyond the age of 16-plus whether this is delivered in school or elsewhere. The probability that supported self-study, distance learning, and study through the medium of information technology are likely to be important routes to a learning culture should not be missed in the evolution of GCSE.

THE JAPANESE SYSTEMS OF PROGRESSION AND EXAMINATION

Before we look at the examination system itself, the context in which it operates will be worth some consideration.

Japanese children begin schooling at the age of 6 in primary school, although a high proportion (about 70 per cent) now attend fee-paying kindergarten before this age. At the age of 12 they move on to lower-secondary school where they remain until the end of compulsory education at 15. As we have noted, nearly all, 94 or 95 per cent, then go on to upper-secondary school where they remain, typically, for the next three years. Thus the drop-out rate before the age of 18 is very small.

Schooling up to the age of 15 is free in the state schools and the pupils are taught in mixed-ability groupings, usually in what, by comparison with Britain, would be considered very large classes of 40 or more pupils (see Table 2.10). Virtually all children (99.5 per cent) attend state primary schools; the tiny fraction who do not, go mostly to high-prestige institutions attached to universities and these schools tend to have a straight throughput to 18. At the transition to lower-secondary school most pupils attend their local school. About 3 per cent leave the state sector at this point and opt for private education (in Britain about 6 per cent of secondary pupils do so). Towards the end of lower secondary, pupils take the examinations which are the nearest equivalent to, or the only ones that can be compared with, our 16-plus examinations. One point is worth reiteration immediately – the Japanese examinations are for entry to continued education in upper-secondary schools, in Britain, the 16-plus, for the majority of pupils, is a school-leaving examination.

Upper-secondary education in Japan is not free, which makes it all the more surprising that it is in such high demand. Fees are charged even at the public upper-secondary schools. Although these are modest, approximately £250 p.a. in 1986 values (Monbusho, Ministry of Education figure), they demonstrate a willingness on the part of virtually all Japanese parents to make sacrifices for the sake of their children's education. There has been a steady rise in the proportion of pupils going on to upper-secondary school, and subsequently into higher education, as can be inferred from Table 4.2 which illustrates the high perception of need for, and the trend over the years towards prolonged education.

Table 4.2 Educational composition of recruits into Japanese manufacturing industry

From	Age	1955	1965	1975	1985
Lower Sec.	15 +	72%	55%	15%	virtually nil
Upper Sec.	18 +	23%	36%	57%	65%
Tech. Coll.	20 +	–	–	1%	4%
College	20 +	1%	1%	6%	9%
University	22 or more	4%	7%	20%	24%

Source: Nihon Recruit Centre, Shin-gakusotsu-sha saiyo tokei benran, adapted from Dore and Sako (1987)

Note: Figures rounded hence slight departures from 100% totals in some years

Taking Japan as a whole, about 30 per cent of upper-secondary schools are private, the figure is highest in Tokyo (60 per cent) but other large cities exceed the national norm (Osaka 50 per cent, Kyoto 45 per cent); rural areas may have no local private schools or only a very small proportion of them. Lynn (1988) has calculated a comparative costing of fees for private upper-secondary schools at about £1,500 p.a. compared with £2,500 for British independent day schools (1986 figures). The costs in Japan can be kept modest because 50 per cent of staff salaries are paid for by government in addition to grants given for specially approved projects such as extension of facilities.

The most important differences between lower-secondary and upper-secondary education, and between the British and Japanese systems, is the hierarchical ranking of upper-secondary schools within a district. The ranking embraces both the prefectural (equivalent to our LEA) and private schools. The ranking of the schools gives particular point to the examinations pupils take before they leave lower secondary. Each pupil is trying to get into the best upper-secondary school that he can realistically aspire to. The system is called the *hensachi*, or as Dore and Sako vividly prefer 'the sausage slicing'.

The ranking, at least of schools in the public sector within a district, is unofficial and derives from the reputation a school gets from the destinations of those leaving it. The school that regularly sends the most pupils to Tokyo, and other highly esteemed universities, will sit at the top of the district pecking order. The results of university entrance examinations are widely published, both nationally and locally, and are avidly followed by Japanese parents and children. There is even a national league table of the top twenty schools in the country – pride of place, for the last few years, has been Nada High School in Kobe (Rohlen 1983).

Pupils have no right of entry to a particular school and, within a district, there are normally slightly fewer places available within the secondary school system than pupils wishing to enter them. Selection operates through prefectural examinations or, in the case of private schools, their own examinations. Candidates for the examination are required to state their first choice of school and schools seldom take anyone who does not place them as first choice. This means, effectively, that a pupil has to be sure he has a realistic chance of entry into the school he opts for as first choice. This is accomplished by the *hensachi*.

The examinations are set in such a way as to produce, year on year, statistically very reliable results. The marking allows little if any discrepancy due to the idiosyncratic judgements of examiners (the opposite is true in Britain). They test a narrower range of skills within each subject than was the case in O-level and CSE and contain nothing like the complexity of question format, as opposed to question difficulty, that is present in GCSE. There is heavy emphasis on recall in the non-mathematical subjects and the use of limited response and multiple-choice questions is prevalent. The examinations are set in five subjects, Japanese, English, Mathematics, General Science, and Social Studies.

Pupil scores are statistically converted into a standard normal distribution with a mean of 50 and a standard deviation of 10. Thus only 2.5 per cent lie below and 2.5 per cent above the range of two standard deviations from the mean – i.e. below 30 per cent or above 70 per cent. When the 'sausage slicing' comes into operation each school sets its entry limits. The top school will admit pupils from the highest score down to a certain cut-off point, the next from its upper realistic limit down to the lowest score it will accept and so on down to the lowest-ranked school that will fill up its places with the lowest achievers.

Clearly, it is important that a child know what school to apply for as first choice. He must have a very realistic idea of his position within the standard distribution and must have good information about the *hensachi* scores that schools will accept. His lower-secondary teachers offer close counselling on this, typically the parents will be seen several times both in school or at home. Teachers also have at their disposal a document that is confidential until admittance to upper-secondary schools is complete. This is the *Dai-ichi-nen Seito Boshu Jinin*: the admittance figures (intentions) of each of the prefecture's upper-secondary schools. This sets out, district by district, the number of pupils who will be admitted to each school. It is an important document because an experienced teacher can use it alongside the *hensachi* figures over a period of years to make educated guesses about the degree of difficulty in getting into a particular school and can advise pupils accordingly on their choices. Furthermore, mock tests (see below) will give a good estimate of a child's current chances.

Some pupils apply for schools whose entry requirements are slightly above what they expect to achieve. In these cases the pupils and parents may recognize that a year may have to be spent in a cram school to achieve entry at the second attempt a year later. The Japanese call these temporarily school-less children *chugakko-ronin* – the *ronin* were masterless samurai, *chugakko* means middle school.

Tables 4.3(a) and (b) show the number and types of upper-secondary schools in two prefectures and their ranking according to the *hensachi* score required for admittance.

We need to ask ourselves whether an examination system,

Table 4.3(a) *Hensachi* distribution of public-sector upper-secondary schools in Tokyo Prefecture, 1983

Hensachi	General upper sec.	Nos of schools Technical upper sec.	Commercial upper sec.
over 66	2	—	—
61–65	20	—	—
56–60	26	—	—
51–55	34	4	2
46–50	30	12	2
41–45	30	33	16
36–40	2	28	2
35 or less	—	6	—
	144	83	22

Source: Adapted from Dore and Sako (1987)

Table 4.3(b) *Hensachi* distribution of public-sector upper-secondary schools in Ibaraki Prefecture, 1989

Hensachi	General	Vocational	Private
over 70	2	—	1
66–70	5	1	1
61–65	10	1	3
56–60	5	9	2
51–55	11	8	1
46–50	17	15	6
41–45	20	12	3
36–40	11	11	—
35 or less	1	3	—

Source: *Ibaraki-kenritsu koko, 64-nendo jukenyo* (Ibaraki Prefectural upper-secondary schools 1989 compilation of examination papers

which allocates pupils to graded schools, is much different, in the promotion of educational standards, from the norm referenced grades awarded in our 16-plus examination. I would emphasize the following points:

1   The Japanese child has a much clearer idea about what he is expected to know in order to achieve a particular result. Commercially produced mock tests (*mogi-shiken*), several of which a child will take as he progresses through lower-secondary school, are widely available (Obunsha publishing house – annually). He will have an accurate estimate that he is, for instance, likely to

achieve 60 per cent in mathematics and 55 per cent in Japanese. The incentive effect is two-fold. There is the positive prospect that a little extra effort will raise these figures by a vital one or two points that might get him into a slightly better upper-secondary school, and the negative incentive that if he relaxes his efforts the opposite will apply. The acuteness with which this is perceived probably accounts for the existence of the *juku*, the private, fee-charging cram schools that a very high proportion of Japanese children attend during evenings, weekends or holidays (see Chapter 3).

The perception of next attainable goal and most proximate negative consequence are only weakly comprehended by the British pupil, in the vague generalist principle that 'if you work harder you do better' and vice versa. The system itself is not structured to make this as obvious as it is in Japan. The commercial tests also highlight, for the Japanese pupil, exactly where his strengths and weaknesses lie.

As a person nursed, weaned and raised on the philosophy of the British education system, I have found it difficult to accept the doggedness with which the Japanese education system pursues its objectives. My cultural orientation still leads me to expect malfunctioning individuals as products of the system. This is why I have been so insistent upon the distinction between intentions and outcomes. The Japanese system does not produce culturally malformed youngsters in anything like the proportion that our system does. The outcomes in economic achievement need no reiteration and in Chapter 1 facts were noted about crime rates and so on. I have to conclude, against my natural grain, that such a system works very well.

2   The Japanese system relates to onward progression for 94 per cent of the pupils to the next stage, upper-secondary school; in Britain the grading is a final judgment on the schooling of 60 per cent of them. (See later section in this chapter for discussion of possible merits of tertiary colleges in promotion of the ethos of entry to continued education in a 'fresh start' institution).

3   The Japanese grading has the merit of high accuracy and is strongly related to a prescriptive national curriculum. The system knows itself, knows what it is about, and what it is trying to achieve.

4   The Japanese entrance examinations are taken at 14-plus, only 3 years into secondary schooling. They have a greater immediacy for the young teenager than our 16-plus examinations which, from the point of view of an 11-year-old secondary-school entrant, are still half a lifetime away. We may be on the way, soon, to a correction of this deficiency in the 14-plus benchmark testing proposed by the government (see Chapter 5).

5   The grading of upper-secondary schools finds a mirror image in the grading of institutions of higher education. We have seen already that Tokyo stands at the top of the university hierarchy. Entrance to universities and colleges continues Dore's 'sausage-slicing' as the Japanese meritocracy progressively sorts out who will go where. At the top of the system lies recruitment into jobs. The most prestigious companies take graduates from the best universities into their management teams and offer them 'life-time employment'. The upper ranks of the civil bureaucracy similarly draw off the cream of the system. Companies held in progressively lower public esteem recruit from the lower ranks of the higher education system or direct from upper-secondary school. At the base of the industrial pyramid are the small firms, employing very few people, that may take the small percentage of pupils who leave school at the end of compulsory education or who drop out of upper secondary (for further discussion of company ranking and its implications see Clark 1979 and Dore 1987).

One might be forgiven for thinking that the situation in Britain is not too different. Graduates of Oxbridge are likely to find more lucrative employment than those from other universities who in turn will do better, probably, than graduates of poly-technics and so on down the spectrum to the school leaver without qualifications entering the least esteemed provision of YTS. Of course, there is truth in this. Dore points to the emergence, in developed societies, of a 'new hierarchical order', based on educational merit and suggests that Japan is further down this road than we are at present (Dore 1987). However, perhaps, from the point of view of this chapter, the high degree of congruence throughout the sorting process, the consistency of the 'sausage slicing', is the most important point of difference between our sorting mechanism and theirs. The Japanese system hangs together very tightly and, whether, in its overall effects on society, one regards this as a good or bad thing, it is undeniable that it offers clear and unambiguous goals and routes at which the process of education can aim. Strictly in this sense, it is a more motivating system for high achievement; the incentives, both positive and negative, are constantly in clear view.

TERTIARY COLLEGES: A POSSIBLE ANSWER

Whatever the advantages of retaining sixth-form (mainly A-level) students in school, we are forced to consider the extent to which such a system is structurally demotivating for the majority of pupils. If pupils up to the age of 16-plus have constantly before them, in their own school, the sixth-form model, that of the academic pupil, the majority will soon come to realize they do not fit this model. They will cease to regard the 16-plus examinations as an entry to further education and accept it as a final judgement. Even good advice about what is available in the local FE college may be insufficient to counteract the negative influence, growing year by year from the age of 11, of this model on less-academic youngsters.

A clear educational break, like that of Japan, may be the way out of this problem. If all pupils leave school at 16-plus, and there is the possibility of varied courses to suit different abilities available at a local tertiary college, it is much easier to see how the 16-plus could come to be regarded as an entrance examination. There is some indirect, and some direct evidence to support this view.

The indirect evidence concerns the way in which the first set of GCSE results have been interpreted. Major concerns in the press, media, staffroom discussion, and the opinions expressed by pupils and parents have related to the equivalence between the GCSE grades awarded and the old O-level/CSE system. The prevalent view is that GCSE grades A, B, and C are 'passes' and D to G 'fails'. This has been my direct experience from speaking to teachers, parents, and employers. It has also been the experience of every other headteacher with whom I have discussed this point. No amount of rhetoric about the philosophy of GCSE grading seems likely to shake this view. We need to ask ourselves what the words 'pass' and 'fail' mean. The simple and superficial view is that 'pass' means an O-level. At the deeper level, in the minds of many pupils and parents, this equates with a qualification for entry into sixth-form study. Of course the majority of grades awarded were less than a C so the majority 'failed' as they did under the old system. What the pupils received in terms of grades did not fit them for a place in the model, the academic sixth former, that had been constantly before them from the age of 11 in their own school. Reverting to Dore's imagery the sausage was cut into only two parts, unequal in size, as far as many (most?) pupils perceived it. The Japanese *hensachi* system allows many more slices in terms of which schools pupils can enter relative to their abilities and examination achievements.

It is unlikely that Britain will adopt a system of slicing schools, but a workable equivalent might be the slicing of courses in tertiary colleges. Rather than regarding a GCSE grade D as a 'fail' it could be seen as a qualifier for a particular course in the tertiary college. All the grades from A to G could be seen in this light.

There is some direct evidence to suggest this might be true. The Standing Conference of Tertiary and Sixth Form College Principals said that: 'The most persuasive argument in favour of 16-plus institutions is the dramatic improvement they have on participation [staying-on] rates' (TES 9.9.88).

Evidence from three colleges in Essex showed a 15 per cent increase in staying-on rates. Colchester staying-on rates in the sixth form in 1986 were about 18 per cent, with the opening of a sixth-form college the rate in 1987 had risen to 36 per cent. Ten years ago, with the opening of a 16-plus institution in Barrow-in-Furness, staying-on rates rose by 80 per cent in a 2-year period (TES 9.9.88).

We must be careful in using figures like these. They relate to enrolment rates but say nothing about course completion or dropout during courses. However, even an improvement in enrolment is a good start and preferable to the direct departure from education by the majority experienced in most comprehensive schools:

Apart from the Germanic countries, the US and Scandinavia, as well as Japan (more or less), have a common institution from 16 to 18. France and Denmark have both been moving towards it as a matter of conscious choice. It is an obvious vehicle for encouraging a rising percentage of young people to go on to higher education at 18. Equally it has a necessary part to play in reducing class differences.

(Finegold and Soskice 1988)

Figure 4.1 Increase in continued education in Japan, 1950–85

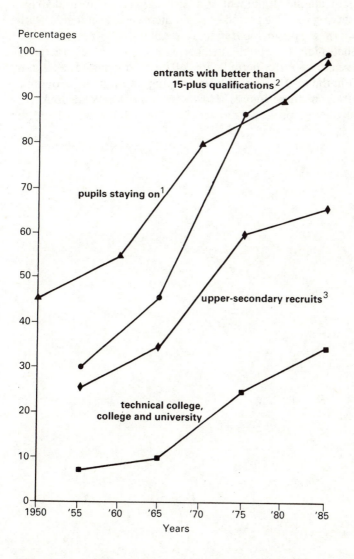

Notes:
1 Figures from National Institute for Educational Research, Tokyo 1983.
2 Decline in 15-plus recruitment into industry. Calculated from Table 4.2 (subtraction of 15-plus recruits from 100).
3 Recruitment into industry – increase in upper-secondary recruitment, direct figures from Table 4.2.

Japan saw a very sharp increase in staying-on rates in the period between 1960 and 1970 (graphs in Figure 4.1). The sharp up-turn may indicate the attainment of a 'critical mass' of around 50 per cent staying on. The period of rapid increase also coincides with the sharpest rise in the Japanese economy, the period of the national plan to double incomes within a decade (actually achieved in a shorter period). It is difficult to separate cause and effect in the relationship between staying-on rates and economic growth from these figures. However, what is beyond doubt, is that economic progress and continued education went hand in hand.

5

The national curriculum

Of all the changes currently underway in British education the institution of a national curriculum is probably the most important and the one with the greatest capacity to do good. The principle of national curricular institution is long overdue. Britain has become a country with a low fund of common cultural capital. By this I mean that the shared experiences in work, in educational background, in outlook, and knowledge are too small for us to generate a common ethos, a consensus, directed towards the improvement of our society to the same degree that other developed nations are able to do.

My definition of 'common cultural capital' has nothing to do with racial background or religious outlook. It is about the degree of transactional knowledge, held by each member of society, sufficient to allow understanding to take place between people and about the concerns of the society. In that sense it transcends special racial issues within a society such as Britain's. Ideally, in an educated world, it would span national boundaries.

Attempts to increase common cultural capital should aim to make people not only more comprehensible to one another but should seek to raise the level at which this is achieved. A longer period of compulsory education would perhaps be the greatest contributor to this. However, ensuring, up to 16-plus, the existence of a greater community of educational experience, through a national curriculum, should help raise the common denominators of understanding in our culture to a significant, if not sufficient, degree.

Several important structural defects have appeared, however, as national curricular thinking evolved. These could be summarized as:

- It does not extend to 18-plus.
- It is taking place against a background of changes so exhausting that it is unlikely to receive the attention it deserves.
- Its relationship to current objectives like GCSE is ambiguous.
- It contains too much material and/or the realities of available teaching time have been neglected.
- Other elements of the Education Reform Act are contradictory to the promotion of greater uniformity of educational experience in our schools.

In other words, a process capable of simplification and clarification is in danger of becoming one of complication and obfuscation. These issues will emerge for consideration later in this chapter.

The degree to which Mr Baker himself suffered from muddled objectives is clear from the following extract from a 1989 speech:

> the national curriculum will be introduced within a new local framework of greater autonomy for schools. Schools will have more freedom to manage their own affairs. LEAs will have a clear strategic responsibility for managing change rather than burdening themselves with the detailed direction of institutions. I am sure that delegating functions to governors and heads and making schools more accountable for their performance will encourage curriculum change. A good system of local management in schools will therefore create the right conditions in which the national curriculum can flourish.
>
> (Baker 6.1.89)

The ideas of national curriculum and greater autonomy to schools are contradictory. LEAs may have the 'clear strategic responsibility for managing change' but the shift of powers to individual schools effectively robs them of many devices for doing this. For example, the possibility of evening out staffing resources in shortage subjects across several schools disappears. Will there be a need to 'encourage curriculum change'? The national curriculum is *imposed*; thereafter the need is to *discourage* curriculum change except at the national level. Later in the same speech Mr Baker went on, in support of the principle of national curriculum, to berate some schools for their idiosyn-cratic deficiencies. Does he aim to undo the work of the national curriculum by giving such schools, under the other provisions of the Act, more freedom and power to be indiosyncratic?

The Education Reform Act weakens the powers of LEAs by a transference of responsibility, over a wide spectrum of education management, to the governing bodies of schools. Indeed, schools will be allowed to 'opt out' of LEA control altogether. It seems questionable whether it is a good idea, at a time of implementa-tion of a national curriculum – a time of doubt, ambiguity, of need for structured retraining of teachers, appraisal, and close monitoring – to weaken the known LEA framework within which education is carried out. The power vested in Japanese prefectures gives a sound organizational structure to the delivery of the national curriculum.

THE JUSTIFICATION FOR A NATIONAL CURRICULUM

A national curriculum can be a great force for good in a society. The Japanese education system goes much further than ours pre-sently does, towards ensuring, irrespective of academic ability, a large fund of shared cultural capital amongst the members of its society. Admittedly, Japan's is a much more homogeneous society than ours; the things they share do not arise exclusively from the education system. However, the schooling process, operating a fixed national curriculum to 15-plus and thereafter a curriculum with a high degree of common elements of general education, does promote understanding between people to a level that, I believe, is much greater in extent, and is at a higher level than in this country. The ability of Japanese to operate quality circles, in which the contribution of all members is high, would be a case in point taken from the workplace. Nearly all the Japanese I have questioned on the point, have proved able to sight-read Western music and make a good attempt at humming an unfamiliar tune direct from the score, even if they could not pronounce the words that went with it. Music is a national curri-culum subject in Japan, as it will be in Britain. Once, having made a speech to a whole school assembly in Misato City, I was astonished to see every one of the 1,200 pupils take out a recorder and play 'Hotaru no Hikari' (same tune as 'Auld Lang Syne') as the visiting party left the stage. Massed recorders are not my first preference in music but the totality of involvement was impressive, even so.

If one were confronted with a randomly selected 18-year old in Japan, one could predict with considerable accuracy what educational experiences he had been exposed to, what he would be likely to know to some degree and the general tenor of his moral attitudes and outlook on society. It is unlikely this would be the case in Britain. Even in my own school, in a small town in Wales where one could expect a high degree of cultural similarity, this is not the case. By the age of 16-plus the education we have given to pupils has produced wide divisions in experience, attainment, skills, outlook and attitudes. We then go on to aggravate this situation with differences in progression to 18-plus, work and training.

At the moment, Britain is almost alone amongst the advanced nations in allowing pupils to drop vital educational subjects from the curriculum at an early age. Until the new national curriculum is introduced, it will be typical of schools that only mathematics, English, religious and physical education will be core subjects in the last two years of compulsory education. Other subjects will be offered in the 'option lines', that agonizing set of Hobson's choices that children make in the third year. This system alone allows wide discrepancies to arise even amongst the pupils of the same school. It is compounded by the fact that different schools offer different option choices. What the school offers, and what the pupils choose, are only marginally constrained by educational needs. The school offers the subjects and the numbers of groups available in each subject on the basis of its staffing situation. Since staffing is as undermanaged as any other part of the education system (see Chapter 3) the constraints may produce a very poor compromise with what would be desirable.

The ways in which pupils make their choices is an almost unexamined field of education. Some will receive guidance and support from parents, this may be good or bad and may reflect the prejudices of the parents or not. Many pupils will find their parents uninterested in the process. Pupils will receive guidance from careers teachers, outside bodies or subject teachers. This will all be of a very variable standard across the nation. Schools may consciously pursue a policy of steering below-average pupils away from 'difficult' subjects which are also, frequently, of vital importance to the formation of a literate view of the society in which the pupil lives.

Weaker pupils will pack out the ranks of the 'easier' subjects – they will head away from physics into home economics; many are likely to avoid history and languages and head for craft and design. The distinction between 'difficult' and 'easy' subjects is not intrinsic but is promoted, of course, by the 'norm-referencing' elements contained within the process of awarding of grades (Chapter 4). The difficulty of physics is pushed upward because it attracts a higher proportion of bright pupils rather than all pupils. Because the percentage of these that can obtain the top grades is constrained by the norm-referencing element in the award of examination grades, the reputation of the subject as 'hard' is perpetuated. The quality of the pupils entering for the subject drives up the standard or, in the case of 'easy' subjects, drives it down. The historical operation of this process has introduced false extrinsic elements into the setting of syllabuses and examinations. To a degree we have failed to ask ourselves what, in these subjects, is needed by the whole population.

At the end of the day, many pupils will make their particular set of choices for reasons that bear no relation to educational needs. They might for instance, choose a subject because their friends have chosen it.

A basic reason for the existence of an option system is that we attempt to offer far more subjects, in the 14 to 16 curriculum, than can be adequately covered, by all pupils, in a working week. We shall see later that this issue is currently being fudged by the designers of the national curriculum.

The British education system is very open to innovation – the national curriculum should make it less so. On the face of it a system permeable to new influences and innovations ought to be in a better position than one that shuts out these influences. This is probably true in situations where the technology is clear and where the likely effects of an innovation can be estimated before it is implemented. Also, if the influences emanate from a source that will bear some ultimate responsibility for the effects caused to the organization, then permeability is probably a positive characteristic. Education systems differ from both these cases. The technology of teaching is not clear and its outcomes are difficult to measure. Furthermore the greatest source of innovation is from educational 'researchers', 'thinkers', and from outside bodies with a particular view to promulgate, e.g. the proponents of the many varieties of 'new' teaching styles which have been hailed, by their inventors, as panaceas for our educational failures. The direct responsibility for the effects of change, however, lies with teachers and particularly with headteachers. Weak central control of the curriculum, the unjustifiable delegation of curricular powers to headteachers, and the susceptibility of the system to confuse intentions with outcomes, ensures a high permeability in the education system to the entry of 'new ideas'. The number of these that prove useful is at least, in my experience, matched by those that turn out to be trendy, faddy, or simply crackpot.

Duncan Graham, Chairman of the National Curriculum Council, commenting on the work of the former Schools Curriculum Development Committee and its predecessor the Schools Council, thought: 'it pursued too many aims . . . bound up with representing every conceivable point of view. The material it produced was often too diffuse and too late. [There was] a terrible waste of effort [like] reinventing 1,000 wheels a day' (TES 19.5.89).

However useful or otherwise innovations may prove to be, they do not penetrate the education service, as a whole, with equal force, nor do they affect all schools at the same time. The same applies to the demise and removal of those innovations that turn out to be fruitless. The sheer haphazardness of innovation has been a substantial contributor to the inequality of the educational experience of the nation's children and to the shortage of common cultural capital.

CONTENTS OF THE NATIONAL CURRICULUM

It seems that the national curriculum is moving away from the allocation of specified amounts of time to be devoted to each element. Section 4(3) of the Education Reform Act stipulates that the Secretary of State must not specify time allocations – a curious piece of legislation. There is, at the time of writing, a great deal of confusion, in the education world, about how to fit all the elements into the time available. A good deal of head scratching is taking place, at LEA and school level, about what curricular patterns, in terms of time allocations, would deliver the legal requirements when the time comes to do so. The designers of national curriculum programmes of study and attainment targets may be free to ignore the specification of allocated time, schools are not.

Table 5.1(a) Curricular content and time allocated

Subject	% Curriculum time allocated	
	Britain (14–16-year olds)	Japan (final year, lower sec.)
Own language	10	13.3
Mathematics	10	12.3
Science	20 (or 12½)	13.3
Social studies	10	10
Technology	10	—
Foreign language	10	13.3
Art/Music	10	6.6
Physical education	5	10
Religious education	flexible	—
Total	75–85 +	79.8
Industrial arts/ Home making	flexible	10
Moral education	flexible	3.3
Special activities	flexible	6.6

Source: *The National Curriculum 5–16*, a consultation document 1987; various LEA interpretations of likely time requirements, unpublished, Monbusho 1983

For the purposes of this book, it will be worth trying to extract some comparator of time allocations, to national curriculum elements, in the Japanese system (known) and in the proposed British system (a speculation about what might emerge in practice). For the latter, in the absence of anything better, I am forced to use an amalgam of sources in Table 5.1(a). One of these is the now widely discredited July 1987 consultation document. It was the unfavourable response to the latter that caused the government to abrogate its responsibility to specify time allocations. Other sources used to approximate the time allocation consist of attempts by my own and other LEAs to squeeze the national curriculum into a working week. Duncan Graham admits that to a degree, the cart was put before the horse:

We are working on various methods of modelling the national curriculum. The only way to get a quart into a pint pot is to move away from the dominance of subject specific titles.

In a perfect world, the decisions (about the realistic allocation of time to achieve national curriculum objectives) would have been made after this work was done. But there is no way decisions could have been made other than those we made at the time because it had to be done as described in the statutes.

(TES 19.5.89)

One must wonder whether the proposed move from 'subject specific titles' is to be done on the grounds of educational preference or political damage limitation. The reality is that teachers, at least at secondary level, tend to be subject-specific. Is their work in introducing the national curriculum to be further complicated by very extensive cross-curricular difficulties from the outset? (See later in this chapter).

Leaving these speculations aside for the moment, the first striking feature of the curricular comparison in Table 5.1(a) is the high degree to which the core and foundation subjects (those that will be compulsory under the new national curriculum) find exact equivalents in Japan. Only technology, in our curricular proposals, is absent from the Japanese list. Even so, there are hints that, in the reform of Japanese education, currently under consideration (see last section of the chapter), some technological elements may be added – a greater use of information technology for example. Religious education is not taught in Japanese state schools, though it may be in some private ones.

The national curricular time allocations in Table 5.1(a) were never more than notional. Table 5.1(b) shows a more realistic attempt to achieve a time fit to cover not only national curricular requirements but GCSE as well. Here problems abound. Not least is the fact that, realistically, most pupils will be able to take only two out of history, geography, a modern foreign language, art, and music (and in Wales, Welsh) to GCSE. The subjects they do not choose to follow to this level will each receive, on this curricular model and others like it, only a weekly 2-period allocation attempting to meet national curriculum attainment targets. One has to ask whether this is meaningful education.

Three subjects to which the British government has given the greatest emphasis, English, Mathematics and Science – the core subjects – are worth closer scrutiny. English and Maths are likely to receive 30 per cent less teaching time, under the new proposals, than they do in Japan. Most schools currently, in Britain, operate a 40-period week (or 20 double periods), and it is normal to allocate 5 or 6 periods ($12\frac{1}{2}$ to 15 per cent) to each of these subjects. The new proposals might actually reduce the amount of teaching time by up to 33 per cent (from 15 to 10 per

Table 5.1(b) A practical attempt to fit national curriculum and GCSE requirements into a working-week of 40 periods

English	Maths	Science	Technology	PSE (inc. RE)	PE	
5	5	8	4	2	2	= 26 periods
Modular* humanities	Modern language	Art	Music			
4 (or 2 + 2)	2	2	2			= 10 periods

Option A** (choose 1 only)	Option B (choose 1 only)	
additional History	(additional History)***	
(additional Geography)	additional Geography	
additional Language	(additional Language)	
(additional Art)	additional Art	
additional Music	(additional Music)	
←———— Business studies ————→		
←———— Economics ————→		
2	2	= 4 periods
Total		= 40 periods

Source: LEA Working Party, author and others (unpublished)

Notes:

* modular humanities is a combined history and geography provision of 4 periods or 2 periods of each separately

** the options provide add on capability so that two subjects receiving only a 2 period allocation in the second line can be made up to GCSE

*** brackets indicate that the subject may appear in only one option line rather than 2 depending on staffing capability

It will be clear that, in Wales, the necessity to teach Welsh in addition to a modern foreign language is a severe additional burden.

Some sources suggest only a 4-period allocation to maths and English: i.e. less than the usual present provision.

cent allocation). We saw in Chapter 3 that Britain is falling far behind Japan in mathematical standards. We also have a lower literacy rate. It is very difficult to understand why government has introduced a curriculum that might result in such a cut.

The portion of time allocated to science was derived from the document *Science 5–16: a Statement of Policy* (1985) which took the unusual step of setting a maximum science allocation for pupils without setting a minimum. However, it appeared to 'emerge' informally, over the next year or so, that the maximum was also to be regarded as a minimum. It was not until the designers of the national curriculum proposals were confronted with the task of reconciling the conflicting claims of many subject pressure groups, that any possibility of flexibility in the science allocation arose. The national curriculum Science Working Group, taking *Science 5–16*, as its guideline, in its proposals to the Secretaries of State, suggests that:

> the identification of precise time allocations for each year of scientific study is unhelpful and possibly restrictive. It is, however, unlikely that schools can achieve the required breadth of study in elements of Physics, Chemistry, Biology and Earth Sciences, and provide for the development of scientific skills, in less than one-sixth of overall curriculum time across years 1–5 of secondary school.
>
> (National Curriculum Working Group on Science 1988 August)

This suggestion, that rather dilutes the degree of prescription in the national curriculum, drew the following remark from the Secretaries of State, opening up the possibility for even further dilution:

> We doubt whether it is realistic to expect all pupils to spend as much as 20 per cent of their time on science in years 4 and 5, leading to a double GCSE certificate. We therefore propose that the science framework be further considered to identify the key elements . . . which some pupils might cover in about 12.5 per cent of total curriculum time in years 4 and 5, leading to a single GCSE certificate.
>
> (ibid.)

This late intervention by Mr Baker, when the task of the working group was all but done, provoked an irritated response from Professor Jeff Thompson, chairman of the working group: 'We operated within the policies of the DES on the National Curriculum 5–16, the Association for Science Education and Her Majesty's Inspectorate. That led to the notion of 20 per cent science for all' (TES 9.9.88).

Perhaps Mr Baker was making a belated recognition of a stark reality in opening up the possibility of a lower allocation. It is very doubtful whether there are enough science teachers available to deliver even $12\frac{1}{2}$ per cent for all, let alone 20 per cent, nor are there any reasons to expect an improvement in the supply (TES 9.9.88).

There is an interesting sidelight on the origins of the 20 per cent figure. Dr Jeff Kirkham, director of Secondary Science Curriculum Review, arguing that the double certificate in science would provide a broad education for all, went on to say that it was the minimum standard needed to keep A-level options open and this could not be done in less time than the 20 per cent allocation (TES 9.9. 88).

Dr Kirkham, of course, had to confront realities as they exist; nevertheless this is a further example of the needs of A-level intruding upon, and introducing an unnecessary constraint into the considerations of general education. A broad education continuing compulsorily to 18-plus would remove such a constraint and allow a much fuller development of the scientific literacy of the population. In Chapter 3, Britain's failure to match Japan's staying on rates was discussed and much of the blame for this attributed to the existence of A-level. We shall see that upper-secondary pupils in Japan, even those intending entry into arts faculties of universities, continue the study of science begun in lower secondary school (see later section of this chapter and Table 5.3).

It seems probable that, in practice, most British pupils will receive more science than their Japanese counterparts even if the Secretary of State has introduced a divisive system where a minority will get slightly less..

In his North of England Conference speech Mr Baker quoted HMI condemnation of some schools: 'Few schemes [in these schools] show how pupils' work can be sequenced . . . Issues of continuity and progression . . . need high priority. Many subjects need to rethink the common experience which should be available to all pupils' (Baker 6.1.89).

Mr Baker seemed to throw the high-minded ideas, that prompted him to make these remarks, out of the window when he decided that a two-tier science provision would be available. The carefully thought out and mutually contributary science attainment targets, which ensured the sequencing and progression Mr Baker admired, were hacked about to fit the lesser provision. The simple expedient adopted was to cut out a number of the attainment targets and the learning content they represent.

In terms simply of national economic need, the supporters of

20 per cent curriculum time for science may be perpetuating a misconception by giving a slightly too high science allocation. Britain does not have a scientific failure. Our pure science can stand comparison with that of most countries, and indeed we compare favourably with Japan. Britain's chronic shortfall has been in the ability to capitalize on scientific discovery. It is arguable, with only the economic intention in mind, that we could afford a smaller science allocation in years 4 and 5 of secondary school to provide more time for other subjects, especially perhaps maths, English and foreign languages. There is, however, a saving grace here. Many of the very brightest pupils who may, under the old system, have been en route to the scientific elite and have opted for three separate sciences (up to $37\frac{1}{2}$ per cent of curriculum time), are constrained by the proposals into a more balanced curriculum. Time is saved for other subjects vital to their capacity to contribute to the economic need to compete with Japan and other successful economies.

However, what is very welcome, from the point of view of helping to develop a common cultural capital in the population, is that all should become scientifically literate to the degree permitted by education to 16-plus and the ability of each pupil to learn and benefit. The present system, that the national curriculum will replace, does nothing to ensure that all pupils continue science studies up to the age of 16-plus. Large numbers of pupils drop science altogether; many drop one or more branches of science – there is a quite high drop-out of girls from physics, for example – and the time devoted to science varies widely from school to school. The national curriculum proposals come out strongly in favour of combined science. This exactly replicates the provision in Japan and in most OECD countries.

Britain has been, historically, very poor at the provision of foreign languages. We stuck doggedly, until recent times, to the teaching of a language understood nowhere but in the British classroom – the notorious O-level French, a written, grammar-bound, semi-dead language that was the preserve of an elite group of pupils, a majority of whom were girls. It is good to see that foreign languages are now to be provided for all pupils. It is possible that the pressure of having to teach languages to the whole ability range, including the very weakest for whom a grammatical approach is quite out of court, will add to the impetus given by GCSE to improve teaching methods further. We should not be deterred in this expectation by the experience in Japan where the teaching of English has, if anything, been even worse than our attempts at French. The overwhelming majority of the Japanese, of my acquaintance, remember English lessons with dismay – some cannot recall a single occasion when the language was spoken in the classroom.

English teaching, more often than not, was confined to written exercises presented in a form more reminiscent of crossword clues than living language. Below is an example of teaching 'translation skills'. I find this sort of puzzle difficult to do even in my own language. The objective is to produce a properly ordered English sentence. It is difficult to see the point of offering a jumbled sentence order that relates to neither language. Japanese syntax differs sufficiently from English to constitute a quite adequate puzzle without further obfuscation.

Sensei ga hanshite kudasatta monogatari wa totemo omoshi-rokatta. (1 us, 2 was, 3 our teacher, 4 the story, 5 very, 6 told,) interesting.

Source: Zenmondaishu. 3-Kyu
(first line transcribed from written Japanese for this book)

Repetition of this kind of exercise is hardly likely to dispose either the mind or the tongue to construct English sentences with any kind of conversational fluency. Those Japanese who can speak English now, have often learned it subsequent to leaving school, frequently under some imperative connected with their employment or in higher education or in private tuition. There is an insatiable demand for native English-speaking private tutors. Whole columns of wanted ads appear in the press.

The Japanese education system recognizes the defect in foreign-language teaching and there are proposals to reform the delivery. No doubt the greatest obstacle to improvement will be the vested interest of traditionally-minded teachers determined to preserve the cherished ways of performing their jobs. This was certainly, until very recently, the case in Britain.

One serious defect of foreign-language teaching in Britain is the overwhelming preponderance of French. The *Times Educational Supplement* (2.9.88) figures for GCSE entries show 238,132 for French; 68,675 for German and 17,448 for Spanish. However, in terms of numbers of speakers, Spanish is the world's fastest-growing language, Japanese is arguably the language of the future as far as trade and commerce are concerned, Chinese will emerge as a great asset.

I might appear to be in danger of some self-contradiction in proposing a wider range of languages on offer in schools. Is this not opposed to the notion of common cultural capital? I would argue that it is not. The acquisition of a foreign language is the important cultural asset, it matters less what language it is. A diversity of languages available is a practical national asset. Until recently the Japanese have been fortunate; both the common cultural asset and the practical specific have coincided. It was overwhelmingly important, to the national economy, that English be taught; other languages mattered much less. The vast American market was the target of a very large proportion of Japan's exports; English was the world's premier language and a lingua franca of a kind. It is surprising, therefore, that the known deficiencies in the teaching methods in English were so long neglected. Now, Japan, like Britain, has a problem. An increasing proportion of trade is with non-English-speaking countries – particularly with the newly industrializing countries of the Pacific basin. Will Korean, Chinese (in x varieties!) and Spanish needed for South America be brought into the Japanese curriculum? Or will the need, as it was for properly taught English, be met from outside the school system?

The National Curriculum 5–16: a Consultation Document (1987) lists eleven subjects which might be added to an individual pupil's or school's curriculum, for instance, at GCSE level. A second foreign language, home economics, business studies, science (incomprehensibly!) and others would be at the discretion of schools. Accepting the philosophy behind the construction of a national curriculum, for my own part, I can see no pressing need to leave this discretionary area. Can an area of study be so vital, to one school or to one child, that the same need is not felt by all schools and all children? If one accepts that it can, then one ought to oppose the introduction of a national curriculum in any shape or form. The compromise between compulsion and choice is spurious. The real justification for the additional subjects might be the practical one: we have the teachers, what are we going to do with them?

One very welcome feature of the national curriculum proposals is that they cover the whole range of education from 5–16. Thus, it should be much easier to achieve transition from primary to secondary school. A secondary school normally accepts pupils from a number of contributary primaries. It does not follow that any policy on common standards or curriculum exists between the cluster of headteachers concerned. Each, being autonomous, is free to make independent decisions. In many cases, of course, heads and teachers have worked together to formulate some common policies and to construct 'transitional syllabuses'. Even in these cases, however, it is the common experience of year 1 teachers in secondary schools that wide diversity exists in the educational experience of the intake from each of the contributory schools. These localized attempts to formulate common policies, however, contribute nothing to an overall national picture of coherent education. Furthermore, under the 1980 education act parents are entitled to send their children to schools outside the catchment – a provision strengthened in the 1986 and 1988 acts. Thus a secondary school may receive pupils from a primary that has not been involved in the local consensus on contents and standards.

Japan's national curriculum also applies, of course, to primary schools. Japan has benefited from the coherence between the primary–lower secondary and lower–upper secondary transition. Japanese teachers at the two intake points have not had to waste time in the remediation of elements missing from the experience of individual pupils as is the case for first year secondary teachers in Britain, and to a lesser extent for first year junior school teachers where several autonomous infant schools contribute pupils.

It can be seen from Table 5.2 that Japanese primary schools run a rather well balanced curriculum. The slightly heavy apparent emphasis on the native language would, I think, be echoed in British schools. This is the time when children are developing their basic reading and writing skills. There is a special difficulty here for Japanese children. The Japanese writing system is extremely cumbersome to use and exceptionally difficult to learn, consisting not only of about two thousand Chinese characters, each of which has a number of possible meanings and pronunciations in everyday use, but also of two phonetic syllabaries that are used in conjunction with the characters.

Both Tables 5.1 and 5.2 contain the element 'moral education' within the Japanese curriculum. The nearest British equivalents might be found in personal and social (and health) education (PSE) and in elements of religious education. The Japanese curriculum has been much more specific in what it is attempting to achieve in moral education.

Table 5.2 Allocation of curriculum 'hours'* in Japanese primary schools

Subject	Grade 1 6-year olds	%	Grade 6 12-year olds	% approx
Japanese	272	32	210	21
Social studies	68	8	105	10
Arithmetic	136	16	175	16
Science	68	8	105	10
Music	68	8	70	7
Arts/handicrafts	68	8	70	7
Home making	—	—	70	7
Physical education	102	12	105	10
Moral education	34	4	35	3
Special activities	34	4	70	7
Total 'class hours'	850		1,015	
Real time (1)	638		762	

Source: Adapted from National Institute for Educational Research Tokyo 1983

Note: * An hour is defined as a class period of 45 minutes

MORAL EDUCATION IN THE NATIONAL CURRICULUM

The only curricular requirement under the 1944 Education Act related to the inclusion of religious education. Even so, the amount of time to be devoted to this, and the nature of the content were unspecified. In those days it would have been a natural assumption that the teaching would be heavily biased towards, if not exclusively based in, Christianity. The Education Reform Act sections 6 and 7 reinforce the 1944 Act by the insistence on religious education and the collective worship that shall be 'wholly or mainly of a broadly Christian character' (section 7.1). However, in modern Britain, we cannot assume that moral education should be based in Christian teaching. Our society is much more divided in its readiness to accept the validity of Christian theology or authority over the moral climate. In addition, large ethnic minorities specifically reject Christianity in favour of other religions.

There has been a welcome and healthy tendency in schools to teach religion as a comparative discipline in which all pupils can participate. This has gone hand in hand with a growing, and proper reluctance on the part of many RE teachers to 'push' the Christian message.

Moral awareness, I think, was assumed, under the 1944

Table 5.3 Credit requirements in upper-secondary general courses

Subject	Number of credits required		
	Graduation from upper secondary	Entry to arts depts university	Entry to science depts university
Japanese I	4	5	5
Japanese II	—	5	4
Modern Japanese	—	3	4
Classical Japanese	—	3	—
Contemporary society	4	4	4
Geography and Japanese history	—	—	5
Japanese history	—	}	—
World history	—	} 10	—
Geography	—	}	—
Politics and economy	—	2	2
Mathematics I	4	5	5
Algebra and geometry	—	5	5
Basic analysis	—	4	5
Calculus	—	—	3
Science I	4	4	4
Science II	—	2	—
Chemistry and biology	—	5	—
Chemistry	—	—	6
Physics	—	—	6
		Both	
Health	2	2	
PE	7–9	7	
Music I	}	}	
Fine arts I	} 2	} 3	
Calligraphy	}	}	
English		17	
General home economics		4	
Additional credits		6	
Homeroom activities		3	
Club activities		3	
Total	27–29*	102	

Source: Adapted from National Institute of Educational Research, Tokyo, 1983

* 80 credits needed including those shown in this column

requirement, to flow from religious education – intention as surrogate for outcome at the divine level. That this particular view of cause and effect has never demonstrated any universal validity in the Christian bimillenium, seemed not to deter the enthusiasts for religious education as a curricular component. Moral education of the young, in practice, is left to the intangible vagaries of individual schools. The views, attitudes and actions of teachers, the ethos and social climate of the school and the degree to which specific courses, like social education, are present or absent seem to determine the quantity, quality and direction of moral education.

It may be that, realistically, we can hope for no more than this. A national curriculum working group setting out to define even the most straightforward parameters of moral education suitable for Britain – a statement of good citizenship for instance – would be courageous to the point of recklessness. It should not be impossible, however, even in a society as diverse as that of Britain, to institute processes that help individuals to develop the moral self. It will be interesting to see what degree of specification the national curriculum makes on personal and social education (PSE) that the schools are exhorted to include in the programmes of all pupils. I suspect a nervous fudge will emerge in due course.

The Japanese, culturally, show less reticence than is usual for Britons, in the promulgation of public codes of behaviour and social expectations. These were a common, tolerated aspect of life under the Tokugawa shogunate. That they were frequently ignored did little to stem the flow of exhortation. In the modern day, Japanese companies define, in quasi-moral or social terms, the objectives and responsibilities that devolve upon the employees, the people who constitute the society of the company. Japan's is a much more homogeneous society than ours and the requirements for public manners are rooted much more thoroughly, and with greater uniformity and consent, in the population, than is the case in Britain.

It is hardly surprising that the Japanese 'Course of Study' should include statements, twenty-eight of them in total, about the aims of moral education. It is as impossible for Japan, as it would be for Britain, to ascribe observable attributes in society to the direct effect of these statements and the efforts the schools make towards their fulfilment. What is worth attempting, is to see if moral statements are of a nature that could help define 'ethos' for all schools rather than leave this entirely to individual schools. Some of the Japanese statements are simply platitudinous, even for Japan. Some, if applied to Britain, would be fatuous. For example, 'Always to behave cheerfully and sincerely' is not only a wildly unrealistic aspiration but one which can also be, from time to time, for an individual, self-contradictory.

I shall pick out a few that would seem to form a reasonable basis for school ethos in any society and have the added value that one can envisage programmes to promote them.

- To hold life in high regard, to promote good health and to maintain safety.

- To act according to one's own beliefs, and not be moved unreasonably by others' opinions.

- To respect another's freedom as well as one's own, and to be responsible for one's own acts.

- To love nature and show affection towards animals and plants. (I like the use of the word affection and the inclusion of plants.)

- To be fair and impartial to everybody without prejudice.

- To understand the rules and the significance of making rules by oneself, and to follow them willingly.

This is not an exhaustive list of the ones that might be useful but gives, I hope, a flavour of what might be included in a national curriculum statement aspiring to promote the moral ethos in all schools by bringing into being a set of common processes.

JAPAN'S 15–18 CURRICULUM

The greatest deficiency in Britain's plans for a national curriculum is that no provision has been made for the period that follows compulsory education. The nearest approach to securing a nationwide view lies in the progression criteria of the Extension of Technical and Vocational Educational Initiative, TVE (see

Chapter 6). Even here, the education provided in the progression to 18-plus can be determined largely by individual LEAs within the guidelines set down by the Training Agency (former MSC) who hold the pursestrings of the TVEI/TVE initiatives.

Japanese students have a little more choice in their education in the post-compulsory period which, we shall recall, attracts about 94 per cent of each cohort, than was the case in education up to the age of 15. The amount of choice does not, however, approach the scale in Britain which has a bafflingly complex array on offer.

Table 5.3 shows the slight differences between the curricula for those Japanese intending to follow sciences and those aiming for arts courses in higher education. In the tenth grade, the first year of upper-secondary school, the courses are identical. Specialism does not appear until the eleventh grade, equivalent to our 16-plus pupils. The table relates to the general courses which are the most popular and attract the majority of pupils. The credits required for graduation from upper secondary and for university entry are shown. The curriculum for vocational high schools differs from these to a greater degree, but, as we shall see in Chapter 6, still contains more than 50 per cent of general education.

The credit system is based on attendance rather than performance. A single credit consists of 35 'class hours' (1 hour equals 50 minutes of tuition time). Fulfilment of the 80-credits requirement is sufficient to graduate from upper-secondary school. It is a basic qualification that might be compared to the 'time-serving' apprenticeship system as it used to operate widely, and is not yet extinct, in Britain. There are senses in which such a qualification should not be dismissed as meaningless. It is a measure of the degree to which the student has been exposed to a particular set of education experiences, even if it says nothing about what he has gained from it. At the very least, it is also a measure of persistence and fortitude in maintaining the required presence in lessons. More meaningfully, assessment of what has been learned is superimposed on the time-serving graduation process by entrance examinations and tests.

Entry into higher education or employment requires evidence of achievement. University and college entrance examinations determine a candidate's position in the higher education system stratified from Tokyo University to the lowest ranked junior college. Employers will either set their own tests for those

110

seeking to enter work direct from upper secondary school or, in the case of local and generally smaller industries, may accept the assessment or recommendation of the schools they know well.

It is very nearly impossible to show what is available to young persons post-16 in Britain because these differ so much between LEAs. In some, pupils remain in schools to study A-levels and other courses, where these exist, and pupils go to colleges of further education for courses the schools are unable to provide. Other authorities have set up sixth-form colleges or tertiary colleges. The content of courses depends upon which examining bodies provide the certification and the inclinations of the institution supplying the education. In the absence of any demonstrable format that could elucidate the principles of 16-plus provision, perhaps I can point out the comparison with Japan by reference to my own school which, I am consoled to know, is not untypical (see Table 5.4).

Table 5.4 Provision beyond 16-plus for pupils of an 11–18 comprehensive school

---

In school courses

A-level combinants (exclusion groupings)

1	2	3	4	5
Maths × 2	Physics	Chemistry	Biology	Economics
English	Geography	History	French	

Possible A-level additions timetabled on demand

Further Pure Maths, Home Economics, CDT, Art, German (A/S level), Music, Scripture, Law*, Sociology*
(* afternoon release to college)

Non-A-level courses

CPVE   Re-sit of GCSE   Media studies †   Civics†   Extra Maths†
Extra English†   Typing   PE
(† also available to A-level candidates as additional subjects)
An assumption is made that all subjects use Information Technology as part of the delivery.

Out of school

Courses in College of Further Education (full- or part-time)
YTS scheme involving some education/training in college or elsewhere
Employment with/without training
Unemployment

A-level candidates can make up courses by selection of up to three subjects (rarely four, in the case of exceptional students). The basic groups of subjects vary from year to year on the basis of demand. They are constructed to provide for the requirements of the greatest number of pupils. Normally, both subjects from a grouping cannot be taken together – a timetabling constraint.

An attempt to define what, in terms of transferable skills, a student ought to acquire between the ages of 16 and 18, might look something like the following.

1 Facility in own language
2 Some capacity in a foreign modern language
3 Literacy in information technology/IT usage
4 Numeracy
5 Physical development
6 Health awareness
7 Scientific thought, skills, awareness
8 Social awareness
9 Economic awareness
10 Technological thought, awareness, process, skills
11 General problem-solving capacity

This skills checklist was put together by a panel of ten curriculum experts working with a TVE manager and representatives from industry and the careers service. There are eleven elements here altogether comprising a very reasonable view of what education 16–18 should consist. In Table 5.5 I have attempted a matrix of these (a to k along the top) against a typical comprehensive school's provision (down the left side). It will be worth stressing that there is no implication that all the skills above can or should be delivered as *discrete subjects*. They are skills and experiences, some of which find a natural place within subjects. Some could be enhanced by the addition of A/S-level provision or by a cross-curricular approach. In other cases we should have to look at carefully planned supported self-study. All should attempt to develop the pupils to maximum ability level.

The matrix attempts to measure the skills shortfall for individual pupils. In reading it one should bear in mind that in the first block, CPVE, Certificate in Pre-Vocational Education (see Chapter 6), pupils are likely to select this alone or, at best with one A-level. In the second block come the A-level subjects where pupils take at most three subjects. The third block consists of add-on subjects that might be taken by anyone according to time and timetabling constraints. The last block consists of delivery through the school's pastoral system and work experience.

Table 5.5 Matrix of skills required against subjects provided

Elements of provision	a Comm	b Lang	c IT	d Num	e Phys	f Health	g Sci	h Soc	i Ec	j Tech	k Prob
CPVE	4		2	3			1	3	3	1	4
A-levels											
Eng	4		2					2			
Maths			2	4			2		1		2
Sciences	2		2	4			4	1	1	2	2
Humanities	4		2					3	2		2
Foreign lang	2	4	2					1			
CDT			2	2			2	1	2	4	3
Home Econ.			2	1		2	2	2	2	4	3
Art	2		2				1	1		3	2
Music			2							2	2
Non A-levels											
Civics	2		1			2	4	2			2
Media studies	4		2				2	1	2		2
PE					4	2				2	
Pastoral	2					2	2	2			
Work exp.	2						2	2			2

Key:
4: sufficient alone to satisfy reasonable requirement
3: minimum required, preferably some top-up from 2 items
2: has/should have some contribution to make in this skill
1: a small input of little significance
Blank: no contribution of any significance

The major constraint is imposed by the limited number of A-levels an individual can reasonably take and that only a very limited number of individuals can take A-level at all. Furthermore, the alternatives to A-level fare no better in meeting a reasonable expectation of good continued education. This makes it impossible to achieve a full skill coverage.

In arguing their case for TVE money, LEAs are generating a good deal of rhetoric as they attempt to make their provision 16–18 look like something that it is not. The phrase 'curricular entitlement' will cloud thinking that should be directed to ensuring curricular *uptake*. 'Breadth', 'balance', 'enhancement', and 'enrichment' similarly obscure the fact that basic issues of 16–18 provision remain woefully untackled in Britain compared with other countries. There is a displeasing lack of coherence in this provision compared to that offered under the Japanese national curriculum. It is immediately obvious that a large number of A-level combinations are possible that do not provide balance in educational experience. Choice of courses is made at a time when general education is only partly complete. Those who elect to remain in school without a full A-level course (one or two A-levels) are even more handicapped. The non-A-level students must choose the semi-vocational CPVE course (it was originally conceived as a pre-vocational course but see Chapter 6) or the demotivating alternative of GCSE re-sits in an attempt to improve on their grades. For those leaving school the position is worse. These are students in the middle and lower ranges of ability, the very ones for whom the continuation of general education is vital. Their courses in college are likely to have a very strong vocational element – furtherance of general education, and the possibility of acquisition across the eleven skill areas, may be practically nil.

More than 50 per cent of 16-plus pupils are absorbed into the categories of direct employment from school, YTS or, of course, unemployment. None of these alternatives necessarily offers any real prospect of ever achieving a good educational standard.

If we consider the eleven skill areas, defined by the TVE consortium, with the Japanese Upper Secondary School credit requirements in Table 5.3 we shall find a high degree of congruence between them. Japan has a structure for the delivery through specific subjects. There is no organizational contradiction between what is desirable and what is provided. The British contradiction, between the demands of TVE progression (or what could reasonably be demanded of any good educational provision) and the existence of courses like A-level, that make the attainment of these demands very difficult to structure, must seem strange to an outside observer. The questions this conundrum provoked in the minds of a group of visiting Japanese teachers are listed below:

● Why is it possible for one body (TVE consortium) to set requirements that the existing system cannot provide?

- Do most British teachers believe that something like the eleven skill areas would be a good form of education? If they do why is the present provision not changed?
- Will all schools or consortia adopt the eleven skill areas or something like them?
- Will the national curriculum be extended to pupils aged 16–18? Is it likely at that time that A-level will remain?
- Does this sort of problem not make it very difficult to manage the schools and difficult for students to understand?
- I can't understand why you are making your problems so difficult to solve. Can you explain that to me?

(Oral questions put to author. The visiting Japanese team has produced a summary of its observations in *Dai 1-Kai, Wakute Kyouin Kaigai Hakken Rengo Okoku Dan, Kenkyuu Hokokusho*, 1988).

TESTING IN THE NATIONAL CURRICULUM

Some of the most contentious proposals within the Education Reform Act relate to testing at 'benchmark' ages of 7, 11, 14, and 16. The age 16 attainment targets, for most pupils, will of course be supplemented (confused? obfuscated?) by GCSE; the dispute has raged around the tests at younger ages. Opponents have raised a number of charges against the principle of testing. The National Curriculum Task Group on Assessment and Testing, TGAT, lists these as:

1 They would demotivate the weaker pupils by labelling them as 'failures' from an early age.

TGAT's response to this is that with careful alignment with the national curriculum much of the danger can be avoided. Pupils had responded well in cases where graded schemes had been used. Many pupils (especially weaker ones?) do better when short-term goals are set. Poor test results should be regarded as indicators of pupil needs, not as a label of inadequacy. This view could lead to an enhancement of teaching.

2 There is the possibility also of alienating parents and damaging the relationship between parents and the school.

TGAT argue that the information parents get at the moment is inadequate. Generally it relates only to the child's performance against the norms of its own classroom or school. As we have seen, in the absence of a national curriculum, such standards, in terms of content and expectations, can be very variable.

3 They could lead to stereotyped teaching in which 'true education' was lost in order to teach (train?) pupils for the tests.

This has been the most commonly voiced fear by professionals and in my view the least justified. A good deal of blame must attach to some teachers' professional freedom to do practically as they wish, and to set their own standards which might be low by international comparisons. This is especially true in the areas more remote from examination pressures. Thus, in that segment of education where no exam successes (or even entries!) are contemplated, are found to co-exist the greatest failure and the greatest 'professional freedom'. Britain's 'long tail' of under-achievers is one of the worst features of the education system.

TGAT responded to this fear by pointing out that teachers' assessments in normal learning contexts would be important. Externally provided methods and procedures would be broad in scope and related to curriculum attainment targets that all will share. 'The administration, marking and moderation procedures will rely on teachers' professional skills and mutual support, giving them both key responsibilities and communal safeguards against idiosyncrasy'.

4 Publication of results would label schools as good or bad on measures that are too simplistic – aggregates of raw test scores for instance. . . . Opponents were worried that schools drawing pupils from economically disadvantaged areas would be presented in a poor light by the tests; a league table syndrome would develop.

TGAT's response was: 'judgements about the quality of a school should not be confined to the extent to which the targets are actually reached. They should also take into account the educational value added – that is, the progress it might have been reasonable to expect a school in such circumstances to secure amongst its pupils.'

Several indicators from the Japanese example have bearing on the proposed testing. To begin with, Japanese children are highly tested and Lyn (1988) sees this as a strong extrinsic motivator contributing to Japanese success.

Particularly important in this respect is the testing before age 15 for entry into a stratified system of upper-secondary schools. Japanese children enter lower secondary at 12-plus and the important examination is less than 3 years away – under a quarter of a lifetime in the child's time scale. In Britain a child enters secondary school at age 11-plus and the important examination, now GCSE, is 5 years, or almost half a lifetime away. I would argue that the proximity of recognized testing, in Japan, both for the child and the teacher, adds a degree of urgency absent in Britain. For this reason, the proposed testing of attainment under the national curriculum, at the age of 14 is a much needed innovation. It will define a clear, mid-point of compulsory secondary education in what would otherwise be a very long haul up to GCSE where the possibility to drift off course would be high. Tolman (1932) and Lewin (1935) in early studies into the theories of motivation, recognized that sub-goals, en route to a final goal, are important. Research by Bandura (1982) confirms the point.

A review study of experimental work on the motivating effects of goal setting showed that where clear goals were in view individuals performed much better than under vague exhortations like 'do your best' (Locke *et al.* 1981). 'Do your best' is very much the motivational climate that has obtained in Britain in the 5-year run up to 16-plus examinations in secondary schools. The relatively high motivating effect of Japanese testing at a relatively early point may account, in part, for the startling performance differences in international tests (see Chapter 2). This is yet another example of Japanese structuring for success.

We should not become immediately complacent that the defect in the British system will be entirely cured by the introduction of 14-plus testing. In Japan the equivalent test has real consequences. It decides which of the local upper-secondary schools the child enters. All of those available follow the national curriculum so, although the consequence of the examination is real, in the sense that a physical allocation to schools follows, it may not in fact be as important as the Japanese perceive it to be. In other words the 'best' upper secondaries get the best university entrance results because they

117

get the best students – a cycle of self-fulfilling prophecy, not a reflection on the standard of teaching and the courses on offer. The psychological benefit, however, and attendant reassurance of getting into the best upper secondaries must be important. It is unclear whether the British system of testing will have consequences and what these might be. At present it would appear that they are more likely to relate to the school as a whole than to individual pupils. Such consequences may well motivate teachers but would have much less impact on pupils.

Test results will, of course, have impact in the local competition between schools to attract more pupils and thus, under local management proposals, more cash. One likely, though distant possibility might therefore be that the 'successful schools' become able to pick and choose their entrants. If so, the testing at age 11-plus might acquire elements of deja vu.

Earlier in this chapter, Table 5.1(a), we considered the difficulty of fitting all the national curricular elements into the working week. An especially difficult anomaly centred around those subjects where some pupils might take a double portion of lessons aiming for GCSE whilst others, without such an intention, took only the minimum the working week could provide. It is difficult to see how high motivation could be sustained, by a pupil, in those subjects that were not a part of his GCSE selection and were only subject to national curricular attainment targets.

'NEW' APPROACHES

Attempts to fit new subjects like technology into the national curriculum are proving difficult in two ways. First, they compete for time with other subjects that are regarded as having a secure place. Second, the lack of definition about what these subjects contain makes it difficult to assess how much time they will need. The key to solving these problems seems to lie in the avoidance of duplication across subjects. There would be little point in a pupil acquiring the same skills or knowledge in several different subjects. This, however, has frequently been the case in the past. Rigid subject boundaries, and a too high emphasis on content, have often precluded considerations of what the curriculum, in total, does for a child's development.

Ways are being sought around this problem by new approaches

in cross-curricular studies. These are far from straightforward. Staff are not trained, at secondary level at least, in this kind of work – specialism has been the order of the day. Examinations, even the new GCSE, are still very heavily biased towards subject-specific content rather than transferable knowledge and skills. A case in point: it is not possible, at present, for a child to enter a piece of course work for two different exams. Some imaginative writing, such as a study that will comprise part of the course-work assessment in history, cannot be submitted for assessment in English. Thus the history and English teachers duplicate the teaching of good writing and the child is subjected to a needless time constraint and opportunity cost.

To achieve effective cross-curricular work requires massive and very detailed organization, co-ordination and knowledge of the totality of what is being done in the classrooms. It may help to avoid duplication but, if it is done badly, is liable to the greater fault of omission.

If anything, the teaching in Japan is more subject-bound than in Britain. The didactic approach through subject specialism is a dominant characteristic of Japanese teaching. Our National Curriculum Working Group for Mathematics takes the Japanese system to task for this approach. In the list of lessons they learned from the visit to Japan they concluded that: 'flexibility must be built into the system . . . programmes of study should allow teachers to innovate and develop their own teaching styles' (National Curriculum Working Group for Mathematics 1988). These, thought to be desirable features by the working group members, were considered to be missing from the Japanese teaching they observed.

I believe that new approaches will be needed for the delivery of the national curriculum in time. There is a serious danger, however, that too much that is new is being foisted on to the education system simultaneously. There is a distinct possibility that the system will lose its way. Many heads of my acquaintance share with me the experience of having constantly to reassure individual teachers that the system is still on track. This is often to project a confidence we are far from feeling ourselves.

New approaches to the delivery of the national curriculum could be the rock on which it founders. Little fundamental harm, in any real sense, could come to the education of pupils by the national specification of what is to be learned and the expected attainment targets. A premature undermining of the way the teaching is done could be extremely detrimental. This perhaps, expressed at the gut level, is the point that the 'traditionalists' wish to make: the fear that they feel. Radical change in teaching style seems to be a thing the Japanese are, at present, not prepared to risk. Perhaps we should emulate their caution, at least until the national curriculum is established.

THE PROCESS OF REVIEW OF JAPAN'S NATIONAL CURRICULUM

A rolling programme of review operates with roughly a 10-year cycle. Deliberations begin, for the next review, as soon as the previous one has been fully implemented across the three levels of schooling. Thus for the current review:

Elementary schools

1985 Working party (elementary) set up
1986 Interim report
1987 Final report
1988 Course of study developed
1989 Textbooks produced
1990 Teachers familiarized
1991 Gradual introduction
1992 Full enforcement

The process for lower-secondary schools follows one year later, and that for upper-secondary two years later than that for elementary schools. Thus the full programme, currently underway, will not end until 1994.

We have not yet had the experience of review of the national curriculum. It would appear that a system like the one Japan operates would serve the purpose. It is certainly a method preferable to the ad hoc permeation of new ideas mentioned earlier in this chapter. If for no other reason, stress reduction amongst teachers would make such a system worth implementation. Nothing, in my experience, has so demoralized the profession over recent years as the steady barrage of change, and pressure to adopt new methods. A known timetable for change would be most welcome.

Some change proposals that have been accepted in Japan as part of the rolling 10-year process of curricular review in Japan are worth mention. One of these is the institution of an upper-secondary maths curriculum differentiated into two levels. A basic core would apply to all students and a higher-level course for those interested in mathematics at higher education. The basic core would comprise: quadratic functions, finite mathematics, measurement of geometric figures, algebra, trigonometric, exponential, and logarithmic functions and calculus. This is a high set of expectations for a target group of 70 per cent of pupils within whose capabilities it is expected to fall (National Curriculum Working Group for Mathematics 1988). Japanese reform, clearly, does not contemplate any reduction in standards.

JAPAN'S CURRENT EDUCATIONAL REFORMS

The opponents of the national curriculum have been quick to point out that Japan itself is currently reviewing its educational provision through the National Council for Educational Reform (NCER 1986 April). Japan has long recognized that although the generality of education is perhaps the best in the world, it does not produce the exceptionally gifted minds capable of intuitive leaps of imagination upon which so much modern science depends. Japan is conscious that she has few Nobel prize-winners, for instance. The reform council is seeking ways to redress this imbalance.

In its first report in September 1984, the NCER, identified eight main issues to be considered:

1. Basic requirements for an education relevant to the twenty-first century.
2. Organization and systematization of life-long learning and correction of the practice of undue emphasis placed on the educational background of individuals and its adverse effects.
3. Improvement of higher education and individualization of institutions of higher education.
4. Enrichment and diversification of elementary and secondary education.
5. Improvement in the quality of teachers.
6. Measures for coping with the internationalization of society.

121

7   Measures for coping with the information age.
8   Review of educational administration and finance.

The NCER also made specific proposals for tackling item 2 above. It said that:

> Efforts should be made to promote a broader evaluation of students' abilities, based not only on results of examinations but also on diverse relevant factors, and to provide a wide variety of learning opportunities to adults as well as youths.
>
> (NCER 1986 April)

It also proposed that university entrance requirements be made more flexible; that there should be some introduction, at the discretion of local bodies, of 6-year secondary schools, combining lower and upper secondary; the introduction of a new type of upper-secondary school offering credits for each subject passed and graduation on the basis of the total number of credits acquired by the student. The latter would admit a greater degree of curricular flexibility into years 15-plus to 18-plus.

In its second report the NCER put institution of life-long learning systems as the core of its proposals for twenty-first-century education. It also suggests the wider access for adults and part-time students to colleges and universities. It has proposals for improving teacher quality and a more active tutoring role for staff in universities. It is concerned to improve foreign language teaching by the greater admission of native speakers to Japanese schools.

THE TEXTBOOK PROBLEM

Japanese publishers tender drafts of textbooks based on centrally devised subject syllabuses. The government selects which of these drafts it will authorize. It is illegal in the state sector for schools to use unauthorized textbooks. Each prefectural education authority has the freedom to choose which books, from those that have been authorized in each subject, it will use in its schools.

With the security of central approval the publisher can invest in long print runs and the education service benefits from economies of scale. This enables the Japanese school to give to each pupil the books needed for all subject courses. These books become the private property of the child. I have Japanese friends who have been able to show me all the books they received as a child and this, at the very least, gives a good chance that a home will have some books in it for the next generation. A significant proportion of the homes in Britain has no books of any kind. Indeed, I have encountered children into whose home no printed material, books, newspapers or magazines ever enters.

Schools in Britain's poorer LEAs can frequently not afford a set of textbooks, even for loan, to each pupil following a particular course. Sharing a single set of books on a lesson-by-lesson basis by several classes is the common experience in British schools. Publishers' costs, which are subsequently passed on to the customers in the schools, have been unnecessarily raised by the existence of several examination boards and their widely differing syllabuses. A textbook, in order to sell widely, needed to cover the material in a number of exam syllabuses. The book was therefore more expensive than necessary for a particular syllabus and contained information irrelevant to a specific course.

A multiplicity of commercial material competing for sales may seem the ideal prescription for low prices. This simple economic idea will probably appeal, therefore, to a competition-minded government and is likely to remain. The actuality, that it is, in fact, uneconomic, has been the experience of workers in the education service.

The issue of whether or not all teachers, or even heads of subject, are competent to make the best selections from the competing claims of publishers, also needs to be questioned. In Japan the selection, made centrally by experts, whilst not infallible, is more likely to be better in general and entrains the other advantages mentioned.

I have a philosophical problem, however, with the authorization of textbooks, whilst recognizing its practical advantages. The system is, undoubtedly, open to abuse by government and the charge has been levelled that Japanese school books are purged of unfavourable references to the last war (Ienaga 1968). The same charge, however, could be levelled at the West German education system. It is also rare to find accounts, for classroom consumption, of Britain's nineteenth-century opium trade and the misery it inflicted upon China. Our invention of the concentration camp during the Boer war, African races dispossessed of their lands and some near genocidal attacks on indigenous populations in various parts of the world are equally hard to find in our school books. Perhaps education systems, whether or not they authorize textbooks, possess a natural reticence in discussion of nationally unfavourable topics.

Perhaps the problem could be overcome by recommendation rather than authorization. The National Curriculum Council could give a strong indicational lead to publishers about the content, depth and presentation of material, in subject text-books, that would attract their recommendation. This could be done in such a way that it referred to minimum *inclusions*. Such an indicational lead could be prevented from making *exclusions* to avoid the charge that certain content was proscribed. Such a process could ensure both practical advantages and freedom of speech and acquisition of knowledge. An essential pre-requisite, however, would be that the programmes of study and the attainment targets be constructed with perhaps a greater degree of pre-scription than appears likely at the time of writing.

6

Vocationalism in schools

As Britain's economic position worsened through the 1970s, the purposes of education came under question. James Callaghan's Ruskin College speech in 1976 is generally regarded as a tone setter for many of the subsequent changes:

> I am concerned . . . to find complaints from industry that new recruits from the schools sometimes do not have the basic tools to do the job that is required . . . there seems to be a need for a more technological bias in science teaching that will lead towards practical applications in industry rather than towards academic studies.
>
> (TES 22.10.76)

It was, of course, legitimate to ask the schools to make a contribution to the economic health of the nation. What must be questioned is the way in which this can best be accomplished. This raises the issue of the 'unhelpful dichotomy', mentioned in Chapter 1, between those who see education in a 'pure' form and those who perceive the way forward as an increased vocational slant. It is worth repeating that, in the light of the Japanese experience, the dichotomy is a pointless one – a non-issue. The needs of industry in that country are met by good general education; the aim of the 'vocational camp' is met by the methods of the 'pure education camp'.

To a significant degree, however, we have shifted education towards vocationalism. I shall be considering in this chapter the introduction of a 'new' subject – technology – thought to promote the economic intention, which may be in some danger, perhaps, of over-vocationalization. Next, some more specifically vocational initiatives like TVEI, and its extension nationwide as TVE will be considered. Finally, a brief examination of CPVE will be made.

TECHNOLOGY

Perhaps without too much reservation one ought to welcome the inclusion of technology, certainly in the form in which it is emerging from Lady Parkes' Working Group on Design and Technology, into the national curriculum.

I suppose (or I hope) that the mere emergence of the word 'technology' into curricular thinking means that Britain, at last, is ready to acknowledge that, in economic terms, technological reluctance has been one of our greatest failures. The educational divide, operating for at least the whole of this century, has produced too many 'unconnected' academics and too many labourers without sufficient technological expertise between the two to make our industry effective and to raise living standards. We may have started to tackle an attitudinal problem (see Chapter 7). Curricular documents of the 1960s and 1970s evolved a conceptual model that listed vital areas of educational experience children should be exposed to: linguistic, mathematical, creative/aesthetic etc. Technology was not included in the list.

Perhaps most of us thought we knew what technology was before discussion of it began for the national curriculum. Each of us carried, in our mental maps, and with varying degrees of awe, an idea of what it was: factory machinery, space exploration, military hardware, and perhaps some appreciation of 'new' and 'information' technology that was going to revolutionize the world we live in. It has proved, however, a very intractable subject to define in terms of 'What do you teach to children?' Technology does not lend itself easily to being made into a school subject.

The first steps, towards an understanding of what constituted technology, were taken in the reform of classical woodwork and metalwork into Craft Design Technology (CDT), CDT (Wood) and CDT (Metal) and engineering drawing into Design Communication. Here the elements of problem solving, design and redesign were taken on board along with production of a finished article or a prototype – design realization. Similar trends were involved in the transition of 'cookery', first by a broadening and academic uprating into Home Economics and then development of the latter along design and technological lines.

When the Technical and Vocational Educational Initiative (TVEI) came along with its massive funding for very small groups of children in selected schools of selected LEAs, there was an opportunity for the recipients of the money to expand their technological ambitions. In many cases, however, schools found themselves spending money whilst lacking both clear aims and a philosophy related to the teaching of technology. Some were in danger of replicating, within one school, the old tripartite system of grammar, technical, and secondary modern as a 'middle band' in many schools was targeted for TVEI.

The difficulty of defining what to teach in technology was compounded by the absence of nationally recognized attainment objectives and external examinations. It was clearly not enough to set up, for instance, an electronics laboratory because this, despite the lavish funding on sophisticated equipment, does not answer the question: What is so special about electronics that, of the range of technologies available, this one should be singled out? One could just as easily have chosen mechanics or pneumatics and many TVEI schools did just that. I have visited a school that had spent a very large amount of money and was very proud of its pneumatics workshop. The mere existence of a technological content area, however important that branch of technology may be – as electronics is today – is not a sufficient reason for giving it curriculum time which must come from other studies. To qualify for inclusion it must offer more than just content usable in the industrial sphere.

Technology, perhaps more than other subjects, because it is new, must justify its place by offering to pupils some broad principles, acquisition of cognitive and manual skills, and a distinctive approach to the world the pupils will inhabit. If a specific branch of technology can do all of these things, and other subjects do not do them in the same way, then electronics, for example, could justify its inclusion in the curriculum. Dr Neville Evans, HMI, speaking to Mid-Glamorgan heads said: 'I wouldn't class electronics as a [school] science; I wouldn't even class it as a subject.' If this statement sounds extreme, I think Dr Evan's point was that, if the subject made no distinctive and universal contribution to developing the mental and cultural acquisitions of pupils, then it should not take time away from those that do, however important its specific content may appear to be in the outside world.

One area of technology, I think, displays the dilemmas more clearly than others. In information technology several options, each with practical constraints, are available:

1 Computer studies in which pupils reach a relatively sophisticated level of understanding of how computers work, computer languages, and programming.
2 Information technology usage across all subjects, i.e. both a tool and a skill in learning and living in the same way that numeracy and literacy are used.
3 A combination of both.

Considerations, in the first alternative, about how computers work, lead us into a philosophical maze. If we need to teach pupils how computers work why don't we need to teach them how a TV, a magnetic resonance body scanner, a space satellite and a printing press work? Furthermore, does learning to programme computers teach logical thought that is not delivered elsewhere?

The second is a much better option; it has high transferability and high general application. To pick up the analogy of the printing press, we do not need to know the details of printing and book production in order to benefit from reading.

Is 3 the best of all possible worlds? No, because it contains number 1 which detracts from general teaching time.

All three options are constrained by finance. IT hardware is now the most expensive of school acquisitions. It needs to be employed continuously to be cost-effective and must be prioritized for use where it will serve the greatest good of the greatest number.

The remit from the government to the National Curriculum Working Group on Design and Technology has highlighted what problems will have to be tackled, such as:

● The contribution it will make to the school curriculum.
● The knowledge, skills and understanding that will form the content.
● Programmes of study consistent with government attainment targets.

(DES: National Curriculum Design and Technology Working Group, terms of reference April 1988)

The working group is asked to view technology as 'that area of the curriculum in which pupils design and make useful objects or systems' and assumes they will draw on knowledge and skills in other subjects like maths and science. A very worthwhile fusion of design and technology, as inseparable parts of the same process, has emerged in the working group's interim report. The remit recognizes that much of technology must be taught on a cross-curricular basis such as the one I suggested as the best for IT. The group is asked to ensure that pupils:

- Be able to design and make artefacts, using other knowledge.
- Understand the design process and the constraints that apply to it (cost, time, marketability, social, environmental).
- Appreciate the importance of design and technology in society particularly as it affects the economy (ibid.).

I began this section by applauding the introduction of technology into the curriculum if only as a sign that Britain was at last starting to take a historic deficiency seriously. Our economic survival dictates that we must do so. Japan, on the other hand, has felt no compulsion to introduce technology into its school curriculum and yet is by far the technological superior of Britain in terms of using technology to generate wealth. Indeed, Japanese schools are badly equipped with computers compared with ours and pupils are even discouraged from using calculators. There is a mild suggestion in the proposals for educational reform (see later section of this chapter) that a greater use of IT could be made, but it does not sound like the harbinger of revolutionary change, in this direction, that is taking place here. If the introduction of technology into schools is thought vital to our world competitive position, and clearly this is a paramount government motive in all the current changes, it is worth asking, in the light of the Japanese experience, whether we are on the right track. What is it about Britain that makes the introduction of technology necessary whilst the Japanese feel they can do without it?

My answer must be speculative and contains two basic reasons. The first is that we have an attitudinal problem that must be addressed before we can hope to make any progress. Britain has long despised the technologist, the engineer, and the practical application of knowledge (see Chapter 7). Programmes of study, in the schools, that might address this attitudinal problem must be welcome. The second reason is less valid. British industry has been very laggard in doing its own training. It has, historically, too readily expected to obtain skilled personnel, pre-trained, either from state institutions of education and training or by poaching from competitors. Japan suffers from neither of these defects.

Herein may lie the origins of arguments such as those for the inclusion of electronics, computer studies, and all the rest of the specific bits of 'vocationally useful' content people have argued for. We know industry needs people with this specific knowledge and these very particular skills. We think that schools can, should, or ought to provide them because they have patently not been provided elsewhere. I have heard colleagues argue for the inclusion of the most arcane pieces of content on the basis that industry uses it in some process or other. The favourite is electronics. This is the school of thought that hopes to ensure that every child leaves with a 'carpenter's toolbag' of usable educational content. That the pupil ends up as a plumber is overlooked.

Such arguments are, of course, spurious and it is good to see that the National Curriculum Working Group's interim report of December 1988 rejects them. A school cannot hope to devote enough time, to even a fraction of the multitude of skills and knowledge that industry requires, to make a significant impression on our economic progress. Schools have to produce the potential upon which the experiences of later life, such as training in industry, will capitalize. The Japanese are very good at doing this. That, perhaps, is why they can afford not to introduce subjects that are thought, in Britain, indispensable to economic progress. The education system of Japan justifiably remains generalist because the rest of society, and particularly industry, is fulfilling its obligations.

Education cannot, alone, improve our prospects economically but it can produce the raw material that will do so if it sticks to its proper job. If that job is understood, the requirements of new courses, and the adaptation of older ones for the national curriculum, will become much clearer.

TVEI AND TVE

Much more specifically directed towards vocational education than the introduction of design and technology into the national curriculum, are the Technical and Vocational Educational Initiative, TVEI, and its extension, TVE.

There is hardly space in this book to consider the details of the TVEI. Its institution brought a change into British education, not least because it was funded and controlled by the then MSC rather than the DES. TVEI sought to connect education more closely to the economic concerns of the nation and was carried through very much in the spirit of Lord Young's emphasis on enterprise. With hindsight it can be seen as having had three fundamental effects:

1　It gave impetus to a fresh look at the way teaching is done in that:
　　(a)　Importance was given to the relevance of teaching material to the lives of pupils and their vocational aspirations.
　　(b)　New teaching styles were encouraged.
　　(c)　Links with industry were given added importance.
2　The importance of technological education was given a boost.
3　It acted as a pilot for the much more important and widespread extension of TVEI known as TVE.

THE EXTENSION OF TVEI: TVE

TVE is intended as the vehicle that will put into effect changes in what schools do, grass-root changes at the classroom level, for instance, that will incorporate into teaching the philosophy of TVE. LEAs were invited to make TVE submissions to the former MSC. The LEAs, in turn, asked schools to make their individual submissions for compilation into the package of proposals the LEA would submit to the MSC. Submissions were judged by MSC officials against a set of hard aims and criteria which had to be met before funding would be available for the LEA for use in its schools.

I shall confine my discussion of TVE first to a general discussion of its positive outcomes and then to an examination of its aims. The details of how each of the authorities, whose submissions were approved, met the criteria, are beyond the scope of this book in their diversity. One point is worth bearing in mind: TVE set out its own criteria at a time when the national curriculum had been defined only in hazy outline. The embodiment of the national curriculum in law means that, in theory, some of the TVE's criteria might have to change – TVE's current if rather informal insistence on 20 per cent science for all may not be strictly legal.

Conceptually, TVE owes much to *Better Schools*, just as the national curriculum and some other provisions of the ERA do. In the sense that TVE has caused rethinking in schools, ahead of the national curriculum enactments, it can be seen as a useful initiative. Schools, and LEAs, whose submissions have been accepted, have been forced to think through the details, in advance of the national curriculum, about provision such as science for all, the delivery of design and technology and the restructuring of option lines. TVE has provided the impetus to get change going voluntarily and gradually before it becomes compulsory under the national curriculum. We are likely to see a convergence, over the next few years, between TVE and the national curriculum.

Furthermore, TVE has provided money to back schemes of which it approves. This, for most headteachers (I include myself), was the greatest inducement to enter the scheme. Comparable largesse may not be available from the DES for the implementation of the national curriculum.

TVE forced schools and LEAs jointly into curriculum discussion – without this collaboration, submissions from LEAs were unlikely to be accepted by TVE. For many schools and LEAs this type of discussion was a novel and productive experience. It is a pity that other provisions of the ERA 1988 – the powers of governing bodies to ignore LEA initiatives for example – will make this exercise less easy to undertake in the future. TVE promotes co-operation between schools where the LEA has adopted a consortium approach to TVE delivery – in my experience there has been a very useful sharing of ideas and problems between schools within a consortium. Again this is under threat from the provisions of the ERA that promote local competition between schools.

In this chapter, however, we are concerned specifically with the vocational aspects of TVE and for an assessment of these must turn to its stated aims.

THE TVE AIMS

It will be fair to point out that, in the very substantial guidance documentation of TVE, there is a continued insistence on breadth and balance for the whole TVE cohort 14–18. Particular reference is made to paragraphs 69 to 71 of *Better Schools*. Paragraph 69, in many senses, can be seen, also, as a precursor of the national curriculum. Paragraph 70 sets out the need for pre-vocational work and work experience and 71 relates to new technologies, economic awareness and personal and social education (DES March 1985). On the face of it, then, TVE represents an attempt to promote sound general education with the addition of elements which enhance technological and vocational concerns.

At the obvious level, we need to assess the extent to which the aims are realistic and whether the balance is correct – time spent on the vocational elements represent an opportunity cost against general education. At a more subtle level we need to ask whether TVE is liable to aggravate the dichotomy between 'pure education' and 'vocational education' or whether it will reveal the spuriousness of the dichotomy. The extent to which positive and negative elements emerge in practice, will depend largely on individual interpretation at the school level.

The aims are set out in the document TVEI (E) 1: in two sections (A), reproduced below in full, and (B) which concerns itself mainly with management processes except for one item (B iii) which I also quote.

(A). In conjunction with LEA/EAs to give young people aged 14–18 in all maintained schools and colleges access to a wider and richer curriculum based on the lessons emerging from the pilot TVEI projects, so that:
i) more of them are attracted to seek the qualifications/skills which will be of direct value to them at work and more of them achieve these qualifications and skills;
ii) they are better equipped to enter the world of employment which will await them;
iii) they acquire a more direct appreciation of the practical application of the qualifications for which they are working;
iv) they become accustomed to using their skills and knowledge to solve the real-world problems they will meet at work, and in adult life;

v) more emphasis is placed on developing initiative, motivation and enterprise as well as problem-solving skills and other aspects of personal development;

vi) the construction of the bridge from education to work is begun earlier by giving young people the opportunity to have direct contact and planned work experience with local employers in the relevant specialisms;

vii) there is close collaboration between local education authorities and industry/commerce/public services etc., so that the curriculum has industry's confidence.

(B). To undertake (A) in such a way that:

. . . .

iii) the educational structures/schemes established to further the aims of the Initiative are consistent with progressive developments in skill and vocational education and training outside the school environment, existing vocational education for under 16-year-old young people and higher education.

It seems to me that there is a very distinct shift, implied or explicit, in these aims, towards vocationalism. Indeed, nowhere is there a mention of what might be achieved by the much-needed improvement in general education. Far from reducing the dichotomy between education and vocationalism, the aims will further polarize the issue. Schools that are inclined already to make the distinction between education and vocational education may be encouraged to go further down this line; those that are not may have their confidence undermined. The general tenor of the aims is a criticism of education as it presently stands, a criticism confined to making explicit the need to add on a strong vocational slant. Other criticisms are ignored.

Sections (A) i—iii and (B)iii seem to contain within them the danger of early 'tracking' of pupils towards specific employments. Phrases like 'the qualifications/skills which will be of *direct value* to them at work' and 'better equipped to enter the world of employment which will await them' and 'practical application of the qualifications' can all be interpreted, and probably will be in many cases, as an invitation to put pupils on to an early and specific vocational track. Such an interpretation might cause schools to go even further than they presently do in differentiating the courses of those pupils who are seen to be 16-plus leavers, and for whom it is tempting to provide work preparation courses, from the 'academics' for whom it is less easy to make vocational predictions. If this were to be the result, the greatest of Britain's current educational failures – insufficient general education for all – may well be severely aggravated.

A demographic phenomenon of the late 1980s and 1990s may well assist the unwelcome interpretation of TVE aims. Over the next decade we shall witness a dramatic fall in the numbers of school leavers. Young individuals, especially the rather brighter ones, will have a strong market inducement to leave school as employers compete with higher wages to attract them. Such youngsters, and their parents with their newly acquired powers over the running of schools, may well produce the pressure to provide an immediately usable, but ultimately short-term-value, 'carpenter's toolbag' of educational experience.

Items (A)iv and v are almost platitudinous. The term 'problem solving' now appears in so much educational literature that one could almost think it a newly invented phenomenon. In a very real sense *all education* is about problem solving and always has been. Education is brain-training and the unique property of the human brain is its capacity to identify and solve problems. I do not imagine I could find a single lesson in a day at my school where problem solving or the development of the problem-solving machinery was not the main activity.

I am being disingenuous. Within the specialized jargon of TVE the terms 'problem-solving', 'initiative' and 'enterprise' have evolved arcane meanings that imply a change in 'teaching strategies'. Here we tread on very dangerous ground; we are in the realms of panaceas, promoted, as often as not, by people from outside the classroom. The current favourite new teaching strategy is 'negotiation' with 'group work' on 'problem solving' running it a close second. Are we a decade away from a new spate of Black Papers as these initiatives become discredited?

That possibility aside, the present is a particularly tactless time to ask teachers to alter their teaching methods radically and to undermine their confidence. Teachers need a safe and tried place to stand as the sea of change sweeps over them. For most, this is the assurance that how they do their day-to-day job in front of the class is all right as long as they do it to the best of their ability.

Items (A)vi and vii imply the considerable participation of employers in the work of the school. We must ask whether this is feasible and desirable. The TVE requirement is that every child

135

in the 14–16 cohort has one week's relevant work experience. The ease with which this requirement can be implemented will clearly depend on the economic vigour of the area around the school. In my own district of Mid-Glamorgan ten comprehensive schools and a further education college will be seeking placements against a background of economic decline – the pattern will be repeated in many other parts of Britain. A considerable burden will be imposed on the school if the value of work experience (an innovation yet to prove more than patchily useful) is to be maximized. 'If the concept of TVEI was to be an alternative curriculum . . . providing general education through activities that brought school and the world of work closer – it has lamentably failed' (*Teachers' Weekly* 6.2.89).

Researchers from Leeds University, investigating forty TVEI schools between 1985 and 1987, found that many teachers were confused about the aims of work experience. Most saw it as an induction to the world of work and as an initiative that would enhance employability. (It is difficult to accept the latter view under TVE when all pupils will be having work experience and the competitive advantage that accrued to some pupils under the limited TVEI is lost.) Rightly or wrongly teachers viewed work experience as a type of pre-vocational training: 'Aside from the encouraging experiments in a few schools, we can conclude that though work experience has made considerable demands on school resources, it has limited influence on the curriculum' (ibid.).

It is worth noting that the Leeds researchers were concerned with TVEI schools not TVE schools. Schools selected under TVEI were given relatively massive resourcing, generally received extra staff and often targeted TVEI to limited numbers of pupils within each school. The work experience lasted generally for two weeks and the support per child from TVEI managers, advisers and the careers service was particularly high. Thus the Leeds investigation was directed at the very schools where the initiative had every chance to work. TVE expects work experience for every child between years 4 and 5 in every secondary school. The resourcing per child is much less, the demand on local industry is much higher and TVE funding provides only one week's work experience. Most employers that I have spoken to, and the advice from my own school co-ordinator, is that this is of very limited usefulness. Many employers are generously willing to provide work experience if they feel it will do the young people some good. A mere week's worth is seen as an unproductive annoyance.

Considerable effort will have to be made in briefing before the pupils go out of school, the work experience will have to be monitored by staff, and finally, pupils will have to be de-briefed when they return to school. There are opportunity costs against the rest of the educational provision by this expenditure of energy.

Many kindly disposed employers have freely given the time of their enterprises to be involved in work experience. Others have proved reluctant. It is worth asking whether it would not be best if industry stuck to the most useful contribution it can make to the nation's human resource development, and one that it has long neglected, the training of its employees. Industry's track record on training is so poor, in the international perspective, that it is difficult to see how it can afford time for distractions like the provision of work experience that, comparatively, can only be marginally useful.

There are some dangers that ought to be guarded against in the local involvement of employers in curriculum matters in (A)vii and the requirement, under ERA, to include them on governing bodies. British industry has been notorious for 'short termism' in its aims and objectives. We need to be careful about a too-ready acceptance of what might prove, in local employer recommendations, to be merely expressions of their current and most urgent needs. British industry, for instance, has been very slow to adopt new technologies. It is possible that the acquisition of information-technology skills could be seen as a low priority by many employers. Those who are merely seeking, from education, a steady flow of low-skill, shop-floor factory fodder will have little to contribute, usefully, to either curricular discussion or the economic imperative. It may have been better if TVE, centrally, had confined itself to taking into account the views of recognized organizations like the CBI, TUC, and national economic research bodies about the contribution the curriculum can make. The insistence on local involvement is likely to be much less useful and possibly damaging.

VOCATIONALISM IN THE JAPANESE SCHOOL SYSTEM

It is impossible to find a Japanese equivalent to TVE; no such programme exists in that country. That, however, in itself, is a useful comparison because it begs the question – Why have the Japanese not found such a scheme necessary for their rapid economic growth? It has been a major theme of this book that the Japanese emphasis on broad, traditional, general education, continued for 94 per cent of the population to 18-plus, has been a highly successful system both for the education of the individual and for the economic health of the nation. Coupled with this, the level of training in industry has made school initiatives, comparable to TVE, simply unnecessary.

TVE is a 14–18 initiative, two years of the programme are thus accommodated within compulsory education and two years in the non-compulsory age range. We shall find no vocational education at all within the Japanese compulsory period to age 15, the end of lower-secondary schooling. In the upper-secondary sector, however, about one-third of students enter vocational high schools or vocational courses within general high schools. We can, therefore, make some comparisons with British vocational education conducted in schools. For reasons of space I am prevented from exploring the labyrinthine provision of full- or part-time vocational further education in Britain to seek detailed comparisons with Japan. However, those familiar with our provision will be able to draw general inferences from what follows as I describe the nature of vocational courses in the Japanese upper-secondary sector. This section on Japan will form a bridge between what has been said about TVE and the section, later in this chapter, on CPVE.

I am indebted to Ron Dore and Mari Sako of the Centre for Japanese and Comparative Industrial Research, Imperial College, and my publisher for an advance draft of *Vocational Education and Training in Japan: A Study Commissioned by MSC* (1987) for up-to-date information in what follows.

Japan's vocational upper-secondary schools

In 1985, 28 per cent of the total number of pupils in Japan's upper-secondary sector were on vocational courses. The rest had opted for the much more popular general courses whose curriculum was considered in Chapter 5 and Table 5.3. Only 16 per cent of Japan's upper-secondary schools are exclusively vocational. Thirty-one per cent of the other schools offer voca-' tional courses alongside the general courses. Table 6.1 shows the distribution of all pupils on vocational courses to course types in 1985.

Table 6.1 Distribution of 1.44 million Japanese students between types of vocational courses in 1985

Course category	% students
Business related	32.3
Industry related	22.7
Home economics	19.0
Agriculture related	13.0
Nursing	4.4
Fisheries	1.5
Other	7.1

Source: Monbusho from Dore and Sako (1987)

Nearly 4 per cent of pupils on vocational courses are on 4-year part-time evening courses and 133,000 are on correspondence courses. Both of these tend to be last resorts for pupils unable to obtain a place in a public upper-secondary school and whose parents cannot afford to send them to a private school. The graduation rate for those who remain on such courses is not high. Some may be lucky enough to obtain an early transfer into a full-time school place.

Courses in the schools tend to be specific. Within the industrial category, in which boys predominate, the most popular are machinery, electricity, electronics, architecture and civil engineering. In the business courses general commerce, data processing, accountancy and administration are most sought after. The popularity of the business courses, in which girls form a large majority, has declined over the years. During the period of rapid economic expansion, companies changed their recruiting patterns and began to take more and more of their white collar workers from universities which were increasing their intake to meet the demand. Thus pupils, especially boys perhaps, were more attracted by the general courses which gave a more realistic chance of entering university. The *hensachi* scores needed to enter business courses fell. The response by the business courses

139

has been to give the curriculum increasing amounts of general course material thereby making entry into a junior college or perhaps a lower ranked university a possibility.

The ministry of education stipulates that at least a third of the curricular time be devoted to general education. In practice about half of the time is so given as can be seen in Table 6.2. There is very little choice available to students other than the option of choosing between the subjects on offer in the social studies block. In all the industry-related courses, Fundamentals of Industry and Industrial Maths are compulsory. The former aims to give pupils experience of the basic techniques required in each industrial sector and to help them understand the problems of, and increase their interest in, the technology. Industrial Maths uses a textbook common to all the industry courses but has examples appropriate to each of the industrial courses for each of the mathematical techniques so that, for example, students on the electricity course can concentrate on questions with an electrical orientation.

Within the vocational half of the industrial courses the government guidelines expect that more time will be spent on practical work than in the classroom. It is unusual, nowadays, to find any actual work experience in either factories or offices. Until the early 1960s work experience was popular because employers were anxious to recruit graduates from the vocational courses. Work experience is now regarded by employers as more of a burden than an asset. As the rate of economic expansion has slowed, and the general educational standard has risen, employers have come to see the vocational schools as producing graduates second-best to the general courses. The increase in recruitment of university graduates has also favoured entry to the general courses and further diminished the status of the vocational courses.

The assessment of practical work consists of a short report by the pupil on the activity in which he has been engaged. The course teachers make assessments of personal qualities such as co-operativeness within the group. Attendance is recorded. A minimum, usually one third, is required for graduation. If the practical work has resulted in the production of an artefact, or the outcome can be judged in some other way, these are also built into the assessment. The result of these continuous assessments are compiled into an end-of-term report on a 5- or 10-point scale in each subject. Pupils are sometimes required to repeat a year in which they have done badly.

Table 6.2 The curriculum for an electricity course

Subject area	Subject	Grade 1	Grade 2	Grade 3	Total
Japanese	Japanese 1	4			4
	Japanese 2		2	2	4
Social Studies	Contemp. Soc.	2	2		4
	Japanese History				
	World History }				33
	Geography				
Mathematics	Mathematics 1	4			4
	Basic analysis		3		3
	Differentiation and integration			3	3
Science	Science 1	2	2		4
	Physics & Chemistry }			3	3
Health and Phys Ed.	Phys Ed.	2	2	3	7
	Health		1	1	2
Arts	Music 1				
	Fine art 1 }	2			2
	Calligraphy				
	Handicrafts				
English	English 1	4			4
	English 2		4		4
Sub-total of General subjects		20	16	15	51
Industry	Fundamentals of industry	4			4
	Practice		4	6	10
	Drawing		2	2	4
	Indust. Maths	2	2		4
	Fundamentals of electricity	6	2		8
	Elect. Technol 1		6	2	8
	Elect. Technol 2			5	5
	Automatic Control Info Tech }			2	2
Sub-total of Vocational subjects		12	16	17	45
Special activities	Home room	1	1	1	3
	Clubs	1	1	1	3
Total		34	34	34	102

Source: Japan Educational Journal

The school's own graduation certificate is the main objective of the course. Because most vocational course graduates enter local industry or commerce, the opinion of the staff of the schools, the school's reputation and the track record of previous intakes to the firm are important to local employers. However, most pupils, en route through the courses, are encouraged to take external formal tests. Many national skill tests (run on the driving test principle of assessing actual performance competence) have grades designed to accommodate the pupils on vocational courses. These are available in both the industrial and commercial sector.

Japan has found it necessary to institute a level of skill and qualification between craftsman and university graduate level, particularly in engineering. Thus were instituted the technology colleges taking students at 15 for a 5-year course. Currently the 62 colleges enroll nearly 10,000 students each year of which 9,500 are male. In contrast with the vocational upper-secondary school courses, more than half of the curriculum, over the 5 years, is directly vocational. In the first 2 years about 80 per cent of the curriculum is in general subjects. This opens up the possibility of transfer to general courses or a cram year to gain university entry. In the last 2 years the courses become heavily orientated to vocational study which takes about 84 per cent of the time. Many companies have responded to the colleges of technology by instituting career grades for the graduates. Two universities, at Nagaoka and Toyohashi, were opened up for the express purpose of catering for the graduates of these colleges. About 10 per cent of the colleges' output now go on to university courses at these and other universities.

COMPARISONS WITH BRITAIN

We should not lose sight of the fact that, commercially and industrially, Japan has been very successful since the last war and this demands that we examine Japan's vocational education system. Perhaps the first point of note is that the education system as a whole *is not* very vocationally orientated. About 72 per cent of pupils opt, at 15-plus, for the non-vocational general courses. It tends, except in the case of exceptional vocational schools, to be the lower end of the attainment range, with lower *hensachi* scores, that enters vocational education. In Table 4.3 it will be noticed that the technical and commercial upper-secondary schools do not attract pupils with the higher scores. In Tokyo prefecture only 4 technical and 2 commercial schools exist for pupils in the *hensachi* range 51 to 55 per cent. The bulk of the vocational intake, with scores in the 36 to 45 per cent range, go to 61 technical and 18 commercial upper-secondary schools. In Britain the predominant entry into vocationally directed education (CPVE or courses in FE colleges) is from the middle two quartiles of the ability spectrum. It should be noted, however, that even in this section of the British ability range, a large proportion of pupils enter YTS, employment or unemployment rather than vocational education.

The Japanese courses are full-time and conducted in schools. Much of Britain's vocational education is part-time, with release from work, and conducted in colleges catering to a wide range of courses. In Japan it is well established that vocational courses should contain a large proportion of general education, in practice over a half. British courses seem to be moving in this direction, many courses now contain elements of personal and social development as well as continued help with basics of maths and English. Such general provision, however, is less structured, and less predominant than in the Japanese system. Elements, like the continuation of foreign-language study, would be extremely rare in British vocational education as would the formal study of history, geography, physical and health education.

Perhaps the simplest comparison is that the ethos of most British vocational education is one of college/training/work, that of Japan is school/education/pre-work. Perhaps the exception in Britain is the relatively new Certificate in Pre-Vocational Education (CPVE), a large proportion of which is carried out post-16 in schools and is not directed to specific employments. It is to this that we now turn.

The Certificate in Pre-Vocational Education, CPVE

CPVE was launched in 1985 as a 17-plus alternative to academic studies. It was intended to have a broad curricular base which, though this would be built around work sampling and practical projects, would encompass a wide range of core educational skills – maths, English, science, technology, and so on. It was seen as the system that would introduce wide curricular change within that neglected sector of British education, the non-A-level post-16-plus majority. It even contained the capacity to become, eventually, the 'umbrella' structure that could encompass both the academic and the non-academic post-16.

CPVE won a 'political' victory over the one-year Certificate of Extended Education, CEE, which many of the examination boards had introduced, with some success, in several subjects, for middle-range attainers. CEE formed a useful addition to the school curriculum for pupils wishing to enhance qualifications gained at GCE O-level and CSE. For the academically late-developing pupils, CEE was capable of forming a bridge to A-level if pupils were prepared to stay three years in the sixth form. As a head of department I even had one pupil who, after a good success in CEE, was encouraged to attempt A-level in one year – very successfully. CEE had the advantage that its teaching methodology was of a kind familiar to the staffs of schools, it built on attainments from the previous point of the examination system, and was based within the familiar subject framework and was thus 'known' to pupils, teachers, and employers. It is not too difficult to imagine that CEE could have evolved into exactly that progression, from the previous stage, that the Japanese upper-secondary curriculum now provides so success-fully. Without too much difficulty it could have been offered at two levels – a one-year lower and a two-year upper level. It had the potential, in other words, to fill Britain's most serious educa-tional gap. That CEE was ousted by CPVE we may live to regret.

The pilot project for CPVE avoided job-specific projects but, by the time it was fully implemented in 1985 the perceived pressure from employers and from the potential entrants to CPVE caused a shift towards more specific vocational inclusions. The controlling agency of CPVE, the Joint Board, comprising nominees from the Business and Technician Council and the City and Guilds, perhaps contrary to their better judgement, included 'preparatory modules' within the final scheme.

Initially the bulk of CPVE entrants were in FE colleges. The pattern now is that most of the 35,000 enrolled are in schools. The local FE colleges seem to be concentrating on link arrange-ments, with the schools, to provide some of the practical voca-tional elements. A further push towards specifically vocational study is the acceptance by the National Council for Vocational Qualifications (NCVQ) to accept, as credits towards its national qualifications, the CPVE preparatory modules, but only if these are modified to meet NCVQ criteria. This will involve negotiations, with NCVQ or with 'industry' led organizations, about the content of each module (TES 16.12.88).

One optimistic development within CPVE is the new possibility that it can be spread over two years and be taken on a part-time basis. It would thus become more accessible to YTS trainees and, perhaps more importantly, could be combined, in the schools, with other studies of a more generally educational nature. It could be combined with one or two A-levels or a mixture of A and A/S levels to fill some of the gaps we saw in the 'deficiency matrix' in Table 5.5.

Is it impossible that we could introduce a 'GCSE version' of CEE, to run alongside two-year CPVE, to provide a full educational coverage that acknowledges some need for vocational preparation? This would lead us to a situation not wholly incomparable with the provision in the Japanese vocational upper-secondary schools. Such a combined course would be suitable for both schools and FE colleges. I suggested in Chapter 4 that GCSE would be more motivating if all the grades A–G could be seen as qualifications for entry into further studies rather than A–C being widely regarded by consumers as 'passes' and the rest as 'fails' in a final 'leavers' examination. In effect, it would be better if GCSE could be seen in the same light as the Japanese *hensachi*.

If the abolition of A-level is a political non-starter, it is possible to envisage a situation similar to the one shown below for post-16 provision in either schools, FE colleges, or tertiary colleges. Depending on GCSE grades obtained the following courses could be offered:

1 3 A-levels.
2 Mixed A and A/S levels equivalent to three A-levels.
3 2-year CPVE plus one or two A-levels or A and A/S levels.
4 2-year CPVE plus 'GCSE version' of CEE at higher (2-year level).
5 2-year CPVE plus 'GSCE version' of CEE at lower-level spread over 2 years for rather weaker candidates.
6 1-year CPVE plus selected subjects in 1-year 'GCSE version' of CEE at lower level.
7 1-year CPVE alone.

There are, in fact, more combinations than shown. For example, within the proposed 'GCSE version' of CEE, different numbers and selections of subjects could be made.

We should have to ask ourselves what might promote, and what might inhibit the institution of such a system, or some other form of continued education, to age 17-plus or better still 18-plus. It is, honestly, difficult, within the muddled and contradictory system of British education, to identify promoters of such a scheme. The best hope probably lies in the fact that we have been prepared to institute widespread educational change through the ERA 1988, however imperfectly this has been done. Perhaps the economic imperative will, at the end of the day, force our eyelids open. The greatest inhibitor to structural change, and the one least easy to tackle is likely to be the ingrained attitudes of our society and it is to this aspect that we turn in the next chapter.

7

Attitudes

Previous chapters examined some of the organizational factors affecting education in Britain and Japan. Perhaps more intractable are questions about attitudes. There can be little doubt that the systems we erect, and the expectations we have of them, derive from basic attitudes whilst also helping to shape them. I am concerned, in this chapter, with attitudes connected with the class sytem in particular. These I believe have had an undermining effect on both education and industrial performance.

It seems appropriate to begin with criticism of the ruling elite and especially with a body of highly resistant, but inappropriate attitudes perpetuated by it. The elite, in the sense I intend in this chapter, is that stratum of our society that forms a permanent ruling group. Strong elements of hereditary wealth, social position, and access to exclusive institutions, like public schools, are common. Frequently, in the past, members of the elite have become political leaders, especially but not exclusively, of the Conservative Party. Others have an unassailable position in the higher reaches of the civil service, the great public institutions and the armed forces. Many are of aristocratic descent or have connections by marriage with the peerage. Others may be termed upper-middle-class but there the similarity with the majority of the middle class ends. They are identified with a pronunciation of the English language against which others are judged for their social acceptability. In other words they comprise the group of people that Henry Fairlie labelled as 'the establishment' three decades ago.

Arguably, the body of ideas, the style, the social origins, the norms, the expectations, and the power of this elite make it the most persistent sub-culture of the last hundred years of Britain's history.

147

The television series *Yes Prime Minister* makes fun of the power struggles between the civil service elites and upstart politicians; the war between control of the status quo and attempts at change. The head of the civil service (public school, Oxford, devious, resistant to change) is able to call on like-minded colleagues of similar background to thwart the attempts of the Prime Minister to innovate. The old boy network is able to strangle Britain with an Etonian tie. Successful comedy contains a grain of truth.

The overriding achievement of this elite has been its own survival. That its efforts and inclinations have been incongruent with the needs of an industrial society makes its retention of power all the more surprising. It is difficult to see why it has not been pushed out of power. Even radical governments have hardly dented its capacity to remain at the top. I can only conclude that the norms of this class so encapsulate the myth of 'Britishness' that the rest of us have connived unconsciously in its survival.

Britain's rise to wealth and power in the last century was achieved by visionary entrepreneurs who seized the new technologies to carve out fortunes from the Industrial Revolution. In many, however, the poisonous seeds of the class system were already planted. They were not content to be richer than the landed gentry and superior in ideas; they wanted to join them. They had social ambitions for their sons to marry into the ruling class. Fortunately, a new institution, the public school, was at hand to help train their offspring in the manners and outlook of the gentry – vocational education of a kind I suppose. The ideals of these institutions, in the mould of Arnold and Rugby School, were lofty; their regime was strict if not outright brutal and they trained their charges to 'serve' as they called it. In practice this meant 'to rule'.

Conspicuously, the public school did not train its pupils to become managers of the industries whose wealth paid the school fees. Much less did they produce engineers from the sons of the industrialists, capable of carrying industry forward from the point reached by their fathers; nor did they produce scientists who would make the breakthrough into the next generation of technology. By 1880 Germany had overtaken Britain in industrialization and Japan was catching up fast by 1900. To the British elites, at the turn of the century, the idea that distant orientals would soon overtake them economically would have been absurd. So comfortable a garment is the blindfold of snobbery that I am tempted to think that, at heart, some still find the idea preposterous.

The ancient public school curriculum was dominated by Greek, Latin, and the Classics – all that was thought necessary to produce the 'whole man'. In the narrowness of their aims they taught the sons of the men who had made Britain great to despise the work of their fathers. The merest taint of 'trade' was soon to become a social stigma.

From the public schools the young elites progressed by right, not merit, to the ancient universities to continue their education in the same vein. Sir Harold Macmillan, in a famous and fond reminiscence of one of his Oxford tutors, quotes the man as saying:

> nothing that you will learn in the course of your studies will be of the slightest use to you in after life, except this . . . that you should be able to detect when a man is talking rot, and that is the aim, if not the sole purpose, of education.
>
> (Macmillan 1975)

In a perverse way the tutor was correct. He assumed the young Macmillan would enter a society of people educated in a like manner. The parochial arrogance of his remark denies the possibility of having to detect whether engineers, industrialists, or economists were talking 'rot'. Meanwhile, in the British economy, the rot had already set in and had not been detected by those with the priceless gift of the wrong education.

Perhaps it is a fact of life, in old civilizations with a long history of stability, that elites are educated in a way that renders them unable to appreciate the problems of the present. Corelli Barnett, in *The Audit of War*, heaps scorn on the 'liberally educated' bureaucrat who typifies the elite:

> Thus in the early 1850s was born the Whitehall mandarin, able at a touch to transmute life into paper and turn action into stone. Hence forward the British governing elite was to be composed of essay-writers rather than problem-solvers – minds judicious, balanced, and cautious rather than operational and engaged; the temperament of the academic rather than the man of action.
>
> (Barnett 1986)

In this century the situation of the ruling elite has remained relatively unchanged when compared with other transformations in society. A smooth progression from the family cradle through public school and Oxbridge to a position in politics, the City, the military, or the higher grades of civil service is still common. Those destined to become elites have changed little in a hundred years. Their entry to Oxbridge is quietly advantaged from an early age by the connections between the public schools and certain colleges. These ancient establishments now accept students of a humbler origin, even some products of the comprehensive schools, but there is still an inner student circle that only the chosen can enter. The right background, accent, manners, and outlook count more than knowledge and competence.

In 1983 the Lord Chancellor, the Chairman of the BBC, the Editor of the *Times*, the Chief of the Defence Staff, the heads of both Foreign and Civil Service and the Governor of the Bank of England were all old Etonians. The rulers are marked by the style of their class which is recognizable anywhere. They have about their persons the visible tokens of elite membership. It is these that raise them to their high positions much more than their undoubted talents.

The extent to which our most prestigious institutions despised, and disregarded, the economic needs of the nation is demonstrated by the response of Oxford and Cambridge to engineering. Cambridge did not open an engineering faculty until 1875, fifty years after our European competitors. Oxford did not follow suit until 1908, graduating just two people in 1910 from its energetic leap into modernity. Cambridge did not set up a chair in electrical engineering until 1945, Oxford not until 1963 – well into the period of our demise as a producer of electrical goods (see Sanderson 1972). There is an attitudinal problem surrounding engineers. The word 'engineer' itself has a confused history. It could be taken to mean a person who has graduated from university with an engineering degree or it could refer to a craftsman working in an engineering firm. This confusion may have contributed to the low status of engineers in this country. The image of the oily rag persists. British attitudes have consistently undervalued engineers.

In Japan, half of the directors of industrial enterprises are engineers and in the upper-management layer as a whole, the proportion is even larger (Kono 1984). Furthermore, half of the top civil servants hold engineering degrees. Japan has realized, as we have not, that the spirit of the technological age resides in the engineer not in the liberal arts graduate. Japan has fostered an attitudinal climate in which the engineer is expected to, and does, take a lead in the formulation of national priorities and the ethos of society.

The British management attitude that all too often under-values the shop floor frequently extends to production manage-ment. Engineers, even graduate ones, are held in low managerial esteem and are promoted to higher positions much less readily in Britain than in other countries. Professor Hutton's 1980 (in Villiers 1984) survey of British and German industry underlined the low status of production managers in British industry. Low pay, poor promotion prospects, bad working conditions and low esteem from top management characterized the working life of the typical production manager. More than 25 per cent of them wanted to get out of it. The British production manager's life consisted of a frenetic dog-paddle to keep his head above water – shortages of components, breakdowns in machinery, produc-tion bottlenecks – led to almost continuous crisis management. In Germany the process was smooth and orderly: few produc-tion managers wanted to move over into other work and were happy with their status in the company (Villiers 1984). Britain does seem to harbour a unique distaste for tasks associated with making things – evidenced by the low regard generally for manu-facturing. We operate an education system structured towards curricular separation, at an early stage, of the potentially influential academics from those destined to be manual workers. The educational spectrum is too heavily weighted at its poles with not enough in between.

Parallel with our distaste for manufacturing, perhaps, is our apparent managerial dislike for technology. Our tendency towards pure research rather than the application of science has been a consistent defect in our capacity to profit from our own inventiveness. The educational system has not produced suffi-cient human material to form the bridge between the academic researcher and the shop floor worker. The talents of the vital middle elements in the educational spectrum, the very ones upon whom the use of production technology depend, have remained undeveloped relative to those in competitor countries.

Up to a point the formation of elites in Britain and Japan are similar and both are particularly clannish. In Japan the *gaku-batsu* or university clique has been the dominant element in elite formation. Japan's entrepreneurs, in the last decades of the nineteenth century, were self-made men like their British counterparts. As industry grew in the early part of this century these men simply did not possess the technical skills to run the large combines that were beginning to form. Men of a higher educational standard were needed and a boom in university education began. At least the Japanese knew this and recognized a need. British managers are still, to an overwhelming extent, under-educated compared with those of our foreign competitors.

In contrast with the situation in Britain, a position in manufacturing industry was socially acceptable and became more so in succeeding years. The possibility for a young man of humble origin to enter university increased. Attainment, not background, was the primary determinant. There grew, in Japan, a very highly structured recruitment relationship between ability and industry and between the universities and industry that has persisted to the modern day. The correlation between the status of university one is able to enter and subsequent job prospects in industry is very high. This is all the more surprising because, in the case of other links such as joint industry–university undertakings, Japan is much less active that Britain (Dore and Sako 1989).

The *gakubatsu* is an interesting and justifiably maligned phenomenon of twentieth-century Japan. Graduates of a few premier universities like Tokyo, Kyoto, Osaka, and Keio still dominate the top ranks of the civil service and big business. Some organizations recruit top personnel exclusively from one or two of these institutions. The Tokyo University *gakubatsu* is certainly the most important. A disproportionate number of Tokyo graduates are employed in the upper echelons of the important ministries like MITI (Ministry of International Trade and Industry).

Superficially this may appear to be the same phenomenon as dominance of the upper reaches of the British civil service by Oxbridge graduates. Sociologists may argue that the formation of such elite groups is common to all societies and that most of them operate an exclusivity principle. There is a difference, however, in the way each of the groups, in Britain and Japan, perceives its task. British elites have concentrated on 'control' relatively unrelated to the needs of the country and on maintenance of the status quo; the Japanese on achievement and the promotion of change.

Entry into the universities of Japan is entirely on a competitive basis. The competition to enter Tokyo university is the fiercest and is conducted across the schools of the nation. Perhaps this is the saving grace of the *gakubatsu*, it does not perpetuate a class but a meritocracy. This is entirely different from the case in Britain where a handful of *schools*, Eton, Harrow, Winchester, Rugby, and one or two others supply the majority of the elite. The nation's other schools, in their thousands, must compete to supply a minority.

Of greater importance to the economy, there has not grown up in Japan the disdain for industry that is found amongst the British elites. The *gakubatsu* members of the premier universities fight just as hard to enter prestigious companies as they do to enter government and the civil service. Industry is not deprived of talent as it is in Britain. It is a perfectly acceptable ambition to make a career in manufacturing.

The Japanese were astonished by the extent of industry, the military strength and the institutions of government that various missions to the West observed when Japan emerged, in 1868, from *sakoku*, the period of the 'closed country' under the feudal rule of the Tokugawa Shoguns. Japan had to industrialize quickly. The nation developed new goals, and with them a fresh set of status models and achievement targets, in the race to catch up with the great powers. Men who could set up industries like those in the West became figures of influence and acclaim. They were more than just socially acceptable, they were the trend setters and the social leaders of the newly industrializing Japan.

In Britain the Industrial Revolution was not the result of national goals, or a conscious policy. Much less was it modelled on another country. In the grand British style, it was haphazard, unplanned and the result of individual genius and determination. The men who made it possible were not at the top of the social ladder nor did their success conspicuously alter the pecking order. The landed gentleman remained socially superior, a model for the industrial entrepreneur to emulate as he accumulated his wealth. Britain had no catching up to do; she was the world's economic leader until about 1880. There was nothing to force a drastic rethink, therefore, about the basic structure of social classes. It would require the passage of time to expose the incongruence between our elites and the needs of an industrial society.

That British elites are often ill-equipped by type of education, background and outlook to take charge of an industrial economy has been concealed behind the cult of 'amateurism'. The elites have conspired to make us admire amateurism, the screen of gentility assumed by people who do not know how to do their jobs. In cricket the 'gentlemen' were the social superiors of the 'players' but the latter were better at the game. One could almost divide British society as a whole into gentlemen and players to produce, in the two portions, a cameo of our attitudes towards the elites and the rest (Coleman 1973).

If amateurism had stopped at cricket there would be no problem but the elites have foisted their vice upon the population as if it were a virtue. We are expected to find incompetence endearingly British. We are asked not only to forgive but to applaud it.

The penetration of amateurism into organizations has been very thorough and excuses incompetence at many levels of British society. It has only recently been perceived, for instance, that senior staff in schools might need professional management training. Until now the system has taken pot-luck that the amateur appointed as head would prove to be talented. Amateurism even spread its enervating malaise into industry, the place where it was consistently punished by confrontation with the reality of competition. Examples might be found in the appointment of people with titles, but few other qualifications, to directorships: the failure to train sales staff in foreign languages; the absence of scientific management in many of our board rooms; the failure to understand and implement modern manufacturing techniques like just-in-time and total quality manufacturing (see next chapter). Amateurism is an attitude bred by the snobbery of the upper classes out of their disdain for professionalism and competence, a defence that allows them to feel superior whilst absolving them from their lack lustre performance.

There is another kind of dangerous amateur at large in our society, one who would be very surprised to hear himself so called. This is the man who takes the practical, down-to-earth view, despises education (he's seen what a soggy product education has produced in the elites) and believes that the only way to learn is by experience. All too often he is the manager of a company. In management terms his horizons are restricted, his understanding of change limited, and his capacity to innovate practically nil (Locke 1984). The lower levels of the business community abound with this type of person. The incompetent 'small builders', the here-today-gone-tomorrow used-car salesmen, at whose hands many of us have suffered, are the conspicuous stratum of this group. More serious for Britain's prospects, are those owner-managers of companies whose potential is never developed simply because the 'practical man' at the top remained only that.

The 'practical man' is able to set up a business and run it reasonably successfully whilst it is in its simple early phase. Because he has been able to do this, his methods and outlook come to dominate the way the company operates. The need for 'educated practical men' is not perceived, the company's horizons remain limited, its outlook complacent and its methods incongruent with the changing times. The company ethos comes to be dominated by 'we've always done things this way'.

Historically there was not much, however, that would inspire the 'practical man' to value the presence of educated men in his company. Up to, and perhaps beyond, the Second World War, education remained doggedly impractical. A 'liberal' higher education, from which material of any vocational usefulness had been systematically weeded, was held in the highest regard. If the 'practical man' despised education and thought it irrelevant, or even downright harmful, to his enterprise, then the educational thinkers of the time must bear much of the blame. British education, and especially higher education, can still be found to harbour attitudes not wholly dissimilar from that of Cardinal Newman who in 1852 said:

I consider then, that I am chargeable with no paradox, when I speak of a knowledge which is its own end, when I call it liberal knowledge, when I educate for it, and make it the scope of a university.

(quoted in Sanderson 1975)

The 'practical man' and the educated dilettante were the lethal combination that hindered the growth of professional industrial management in Britain. We failed to see that others were taking a different perspective. Professor Tony Eccles, of the London Business School, speaking of the present failure to realize that trained managers are more effective in competitive terms remarked: 'Perhaps that's why we have difficulty in Britain, because we do believe still, residually, that the gifted amateur is good enough' (television programme).

There has been a tendency towards complacency, a passive reluctance to move with the times and, above all, a failure to professionalize. The effects of the latter are obvious. Management has been slow to appreciate changes in society which render obsolete, for example, the demarcation of managers from managed. Attitudinal approaches to the workforce, that may have been accepted as 'natural' three decades ago, have been overtaken by social change. 'The workers will bloody well do as they are told' is no longer a philosophy that can be used to run a productive modern enterprise. The deserved response this attitude elicits from workers is: 'Don't ask me to worry about the company, mate, I'm only on wages.' Much of British management has failed to take advantage of the new methods, use of computers, employment of analytical techniques to monitor the performance of sections of the business or training methods for themselves and their workers.

The whole Japanese approach is different. The Japanese know it is better to carry people with you than to bully; they never adopt the 'we're the bosses attitude'. . . . They're slow and very thorough. They're not daft or soft. They insist on tough terms and they get it by carrying people along. The British try to run things by instruction.

(George Wright, General Secretary Wales TUC, talking about Japanese companies in Wales, *Observer*, 8.5.83)

British management has been bedevilled by mistaken attitudes towards, and poor communications with the workforce on the shop floor. To judge from what the unemployed say are the greatest difficulties of their situation – boredom, a sense of dislocation, feelings of rejection – it would seem that fundamentally the British like work and are happy to be there. However, our workers are difficult to manage because of two factors.

First, there is high group loyalty amongst workers. We have a collectivist-minded workforce that expresses its values in sanctions against 'blacklegs', distrusts fellow workers who are seen as 'tools of the bosses', and is intolerant of individualism in its midst. Its instinct for 'one out, all out', often for trifling reasons, has become famous the world over. Second, our workforce is much more prone, than that of our competitors, to feelings that it is being exploited. Management, all too often, has failed to take these attitudes into account – the potential advantage of having a collectivist workforce has been turned into a disadvantage by making workers feel they are second-class citizens. Differences in canteen, toilet, and recreational facilities emphasize the divide. Failure to communicate honestly destroys trust. Keeping workers short of information throws them back on to their own group solidarity, causes them to draw their own, and often mistaken conclusions about change. If lay-offs apply only to workers and not to managers, if large dividends are paid to shareholders when the workers are asked for wage restraint, the company puts itself into the position of unmanageability.

I believe that these attitudes are both a cause and an effect of the way we structure our education service. I am not convinced that the differentiation of courses in schools is a response to the educational needs of pupils and does not arise from the attitudinal psychology of the differentiators.

The tendency to differentiate between people promotes, in work, a cycle of defects one of whose results is under-training. Dr David Owen, who has consistently supported the industrial partnership, advocates the removal of old status barriers and an abandonment of the meaningless rhetoric of confrontation:

> The petty 'apartheid' of the workplace has to go. Unless modern management recognizes this, we will pay a heavy price with divisions and conflict at work, when there should be co-operation and partnership. What is more, as Japanese management has shown in the UK, partnership at work is also more efficient than conflict.
>
> (Owen 1986)

Mr Akio Morita, co-founder of the Sony corporation, is an exponent of Japanese management attitudes. A major aim of these attitudes is communication between people, between workers and supervisors and between both of these and management. It would be pointless to attempt such communication unless relationships within the company were good. Mr Morita's overriding concern, therefore, is with harmony in the company and the release of the creative spirit among his workforce.

Mr Morita's philosophy is summed up in this quotation:

> The most important mission for a Japanese manager is to develop a healthy relationship with employees, to create a family-like feeling within the corporation, a feeling that employees and managers share the same fate. Those companies that are most successful in Japan are those that have

managed to create a shared sense of fate among all the employees.

(Morita 1986)

He stresses that no matter how talented a manager is, no matter how much money is thrown at a problem, the future of the business is in the hands of the people it employs; it is 'actually in the hands of the youngest recruit on the staff'. To maintain this sense of community takes skill and effort and the manager has to care about, and genuinely believe in what he is doing. During the familiar early morning briefings that take place on the shop floor, supervisors inform the workers of what the day's tasks will be and report on the previous day's work. At the same time they keep their eyes open for anyone who is looking ill or worried. They have a duty to inquire into the problem, to care about it. Mr Morita admits that it might be easier, in a one-race nation like Japan, to promote the feeling of a company as a social security organization but he thinks the most important characteristic for co-operation is a high standard of education all round. It may be that a large common educational experience is even more important in the formation of common attitudes.

In order to sustain a greater sense of equality, Japanese managers have to do without many of the perks that British management believes are a right. The pay of a top executive is seldom more than eight times that of an entry-level management recruit. Compare this with some of Britain's million-a-year pay packets. Tax havens are unknown, and tax avoidance on pay is difficult. The pay of top executives is published each year in the newspapers – Japanese managers do not like to appear greedy in the eyes of the public. The outrageous golden handshakes of the West are not given in Japan. As Mr Morita says, nobody in Sony has a 'golden parachute'; in times of difficulty, in Japanese companies, the top executives are the first to take a pay cut.

The best Japanese management is forgiving of mistakes. The important thing is not to find a culprit, and perhaps sack him, but to ensure the mistake does not happen twice. Mr Morita quite cheerfully admits to his own mistakes in his book. This attitude helps to release the creative energy of the company. Creativity, to the Japanese manager, has three components: technology, product planning and sales. Unless all three are present, no real creative act, as far as the company is concerned, is possible. Any one of these, or indeed any two, alone, will not produce an effect in the market and will not, therefore, have any effect in providing employment for the workforce.

Uneasily between the British elite and the working class sits the middle class, despised by the class above it and fearful of the one below it, and concerned much more than anything else about retaining its place in the pecking order. If the middle class had found the courage to stand for its own convictions it could have formed the middle ground into which power was drawn. It has failed signally in this task. As the main reservoir of the 'floating vote' it has been responsible for the constant changes in the political outlook of governments. When its social intellect has been pricked it has put the left into power. When its own position has been threatened it has kicked them out again.

A true urban middle class, confident of its own worth, true to its own values and proud of itself, has never formed in Britain as it has for instance in Germany. 'Middle class' is almost a pejorative term in Britain. It is used with social disdain by the upper class and with academic disdain by left-wing intellectuals who dominate the thinking in the trendier parts of academia, the media, and the Labour Party. The various strata of the middle class are seen by many of their occupants merely as stage camps en route to a distant summit by the all-consuming process of social and economic climbing. The reconstruction of social values espoused in Thatcherism has produced the 'Yuppie' out of the social climber.

The middle class has been unable to form any lasting alliances with the working class from whom it differs so much in speech, manners, and outlook. At the grass roots the working and middle classes maintain hostile neutrality across a gaping educational divide between those who left school early and those who continued into A-level or higher education. This situation has hardly been changed by the general provision of education. The working class is still grossly under-represented in percentage terms, even in comprehensive schools, amongst sixth formers. The same is true in the universities.

When the state, belatedly in 1902, undertook the general organization of secondary education, the ancient grammar school was taken as almost the exclusive model for secondary schools. The educational ethos of the middle class was formed in the grammar schools which, in turn, in large measure, sought to ape the public schools in the 'other-worldliness' of their curriculum and institutions. What, in logical or purposeful intention,

159

could ever have given rise to the grammar school 'Speech Day'? Many of the grammar schools set a social ethos that was alien, and sometimes openly hostile, to the working class. Quotations from grammar school headteachers reveal how some of them thought:

> I see grammar school education very strongly as a matter of communicating middle-class values.

> The aim of grammar school education is to make a rounded person, not to concentrate on exam passing and jobs. It is concerned with manners . . . and the creation of style: the public-school virtues, in fact – though without the snobbery.

> Character weaknesses (of working-class children) will undoubtedly prevent a number of young people from developing their talents to the full.

> (quoted in Jackson and Marsden 1962)

I wonder, does the final qualifier in the second quotation indicate that the headteacher, who made this remark, 'knew' her place in the pecking order and felt, on behalf of her school, a victim of it? Is the term 'character', in the third quotation, a tailor-made judgement from within the ethos of the public and grammar school of those outside it? Is this mysterious quality, 'character', heard so often bandied in educational circles, the defining, yet undefined extreme end of the 'unhelpful dichotomy' between 'pure' education and education contributing to the economic good? Is 'character' the quality that, developed on the playing fields of Eton, won the Battle of Waterloo?

Surveys into Japanese attitudes revealed that over 90 per cent of the population considered itself to be middle class. I have serious doubts as to whether exact parallels can be drawn between what the Japanese regard as middle-class and what we take it to mean. However, it is clear that most Japanese see themselves as belonging to the same social grouping. Each believes the majority of his countrymen hold substantially the same views, have the same kind of aspirations and have had a fairly similar school experience as himself. It hardly matters whether this is true or not. What people believe, as opposed to what they know to be fact, is the most important determinant in class consciousness. Confidence in their place in society has enabled the Japanese manager, worker, government official, professional person and private entrepreneur to feel safe in the co-operation they give to economic growth. From their position amongst the 90 per cent they are able to see that success for the country will bring them their share of the rewards. In Britain co-operation is given grudgingly, if at all. At each level of our society lurks the suspicion that the fruits of national success will go to someone else – to another class.

A report by Opinion Research and Communication, on what workers thought about profits, consistently revealed the following attitude.

> Profits go to the wrong people. They go mainly to share-holders, directors, the government . . . and workers get the least benefit from the company profits. It will make little or no difference to me whether my employer makes good or poor profits.
>
> (quoted in Villiers 1984)

The organization and form of the British education system has left the working class grotesquely under-educated to cope with the modern world. Economic illiteracy prompts the working class to believe that its poverty can be banished simply by the redistribution of wealth. It has fallen victim to the politics of jealousy. It believes one of the most destructive economic myths of the modern world – that wealth creates poverty, that when an entrepreneur becomes rich he does so by the impoverishment of others rather than by the creation of wealth that did not previously exist. Blindness to economic reality prevents the worker from distinguishing between the deserving and the unde-serving rich. In general he sees little difference between the industrialist who has struggled, against all odds, to create pro-ductive wealth and employment and those who have simply acquired wealth for themselves but have produced nothing. Speculators in the money markets, asset strippers, and property barons are viewed in the same light as genuine industrial entre-preneurs. It was, after all, in his study of the British working class, that Marx formulated his notion of the alienated prole-tariat. The times have changed but the outdated, class-based dogma persists, half understood, but thoroughly accepted, in the guts of the working class.

The excesses of industrial capitalism in the past deserved the opposition of the working class. Credit must go to the men, from whatever class, who led this movement. But now the situation has changed. If the British worker is one of the worst paid in the developed world, part of the blame must rest on his own shoulders. He has been content to remain in a state of economic ignorance and to espouse the political simplicities of 'the class war'. His attack on industrial capital has helped to destroy his own standard of living whilst leaving his real enemy, the unproductively wealthy, relatively unscathed. Correlli Barnett does not pull any punches on this point; his words bleed with the frustrations Britain must endure from its under-educated working class:

> Of all the grievous long-term handicaps bequeathed to modern Britain . . . one of the most pervasive and the most intractable was that of a workforce too largely composed of coolies, with the psychology and primitive culture to be expected of coolies.

> (Barnett 1987)

Perhaps Correlli Barnett overstates his case in the word 'coolies' but I think I know what he means. The British working class has been squeezed into supinity by inappropriate and irrelevant representation in government. It has been lulled into apathy by an abysmal neglect of education, both structurally and of its own choosing, and has been side-tracked into low standards of living by the trades unions. It has been culturally black-jacked by tabloid newspapers like the *Sun*.

The British working class has persistently clung to a low level of aspiration that has kept it amongst the least educated, least mobile group in the developed world. Perhaps Richard Hoggart in *The Uses of Literacy* sums up best the non-aspiring nature of the working class: 'Most working class people are not climbing; they do not quarrel with their general level; they only want a little more that allows them a few frills' (Hoggart 1971).

The Japanese standard of education, as I hope to have shown, gets better results than ours. The average production-line worker is of a comparable standard with our 18-plus rather than our 16-plus school leavers and has remained in education in those vital years when the 'social mind' is developing. He is much more able than the British worker to dissect economic reality from the myths of party politics. He has a level of sophistication that enables him to function as a highly trained individual within a company and to make relative assessments of what is in his own interest in a wider economic context. He is a supporter of the idea of growth and an active contibutor to it. No doubt he would enjoy having the same standard of living as the owner of the company that employs him and in this respect suffers from the same frailty as the rest of mankind. He does not, however, make this the basis for his attitude to his work. To do so would simply fly in the face of reality. He is unlikely to support a movement that told him that the redistribution of the chairman's income amongst the workers was his path to prosperity.

It is almost inconveivable that the large federations of Japanese industrial unions, like Domei and Churitsu Roren, could have adopted the economically naive attitudes to employment and remuneration that have been evident in Britain. Could they have supported policies that made their members poorer as a result of their activities? Japanese workers are sufficiently well educated to ensure, through the force of their collective opinion, that their representatives pursue policies congruent with the workers' long-term interest. In contrast, the British worker is a bewildered character, slumping further and further into apathy and seduced into poverty by myths about the nature of the problem he confronts. He clings to the comfort of knowing his class and settling for a standard of living he has come to believe is his lot.

Within the objectives of this book we must ask whether there is anything in the current educational changes that is likely to alter attitudes. I believe that a national curriculum will be a worthwhile contributor − given that it extends only to 16-plus − to some increased commonality in attitudes. At the least it will form the basis of a consensus about what should be taught to all pupils. From this it may be possible for a wider view to grow, in the future, about education beyond 16-plus. If we can break through the 16-plus educational divide it may be possible, within a generation, to produce a radical shift in the attitudes and expectations of society.

That the shifting of attitudes is not an easy task, however, can be seen in many aspects of the current change. Not least of these is a fundamental arrogance that the British way is best after all.

The general tenor of the Mathematics Working Group's comments, on the Japanese education system, seem as concerned to admonish Japan, for not adopting a British view, as to learn from that country. The Group's tenacious hold on its own value system seems unshaken by its visit to Japan. The summary of the Group's remarks (p. 118, item 18) contains five lessons 'learned' from the visit. One of these is positive: the Japanese system sets high expectations and we must do the same. One is platitudinous and should not have required an expensive visit to confirm it: 'the benefits of an adequately manned, well-motivated teacher force are self-evident'.

Three of the lessons are negative. The group is concerned that we should do what the Japanese do not. The relative rigidity of the Japanese system provokes them to propose greater flexibility for ours. The minimal freedom for Japanese teachers to depart from approved methods provokes the recommendation that ours should be innovative. They propose that mathematics should be 'interesting, enjoyable and relevant to pupils' needs and experiences' whereas, clearly, in Japan this is very often not the case. (It is by no means the case in this country either to judge from our results and the experiences of most pupils and teachers despite the laudable intentions in the last decade's proposals for changes in teaching styles and emphasis.)

As a last plea to the working group, before they go ahead and learn nothing from Japan, I would say, in the words of Oliver Cromwell: 'I beseech you, in the bowels of Christ, think it possible you may be wrong.'

I am concerned that the private and public schools are exempted from the national curriculum. The pessimistic view of this would be that, if for the foreseeable future, a small number of schools continue to exert a disproportionate influence at the highest levels of government and bureaucracy, exemption from the national curriculum would leave them free to perpetuate their own idosyncratic deficiencies, and exclusivity, that have been so damaging in the past. I am as concerned about their exemption from the ethos of the national curriculum as from its content. Has the message been sent out that the national curriculum is only for ordinary people?

There is much in the new measures aimed at promoting better understanding and appreciation of the role of industry. In this context the providers of education are exhorted to ensure relevance to the world of work. Work experience and economic awareness are encouraged as integrals of a wide range of curricular subjects. *Better Schools*, the well-spring of most of the current changes, says:

It will . . . be necessary to resolve the issue of how best to fit work-related skills within initial full time education . . . all pupils should follow a broad, balanced and suitably differentiated programme until age 16 . . . [which] should contain a strong element which relates to the technological aspects of working life.

(DES April 1985, para. 49)

This paragraph goes on to explain its philosophy about the place of pre-vocational courses, pre-16, as a bridge to vocational courses after compulsory education.

If I was absolutely certain that the intention of statements like this were directed to correcting Britain's attitudinal malaise vis-à-vis industry and work I should be happy enough. It is possible, however, to read this statement as a perpetuation of early segregation of the sheep from the goats. The mention of 'work-related skills' closely followed by 'suitably differentiated programme' seems to imply an attitudinal similarity to what has gone on in the past. The statements are not too dissimilar from those surrounding the 1944 Education Act, that set out the (largely attitudinal?) rationale for the distinction between grammar and secondary modern schools. Indeed, there is a good case to be argued that the organization of education is a strong 'confirmer' of social prejudices – that we construct systems that will maintain the status quo:

It is only with . . . the spread of a democratic and egalitarian rhetoric, that the school too came to support . . . a concept of 'democratic citizenship' at odds with an earlier concept of 'my station and its duties'.

This, however, does not mean that schools ceased to be agencies of 'political socialization' and an affirmation of the status quo. It means rather that they came to perform this role much less explicitly and directly though not necessarily less effectively.

(Miliband 1973)

No doubt this criticism is applicable to the education systems in all countries. It is certainly true of the Japanese system's perpetuation of the lower status of women, for example. Britain is, perhaps, overly concerned with the provision of *structural* differentiation of learning experiences. I am as sure as I can be

165

that this does not entirely derive from the altruistic motive of recognizing differences in ability. We are obsessed attitudinally with putting people into appropriate boxes. The Japanese are much more content than we, generally, with letting people differentiate themselves according to ability by providing *structurally similar* education for all.

8

The economic objectives of education and training

In previous chapters I have used British educational practices, systems and institutions to carry the theme of the book, and comparison with Japan has been secondary. In this chapter I change the approach because space limits the amount of coverage that can be given to a consideration of the relationship between education and training provision.

Instead of attempting to analyse the differences in British and Japanese training provision, I have concentrated upon descriptions of the techniques of Japanese industry. These ought to be amongst the outcomes, in Britain, of training capitalizing upon the educational base. To do this I describe in simple terms what Japanese companies are doing that we, largely, are not doing or are, presently unable to do. The chapter is written with the educationalist, rather than the industrialist in mind.

The chapter supports the main themes of the book in terms of general questions about deficiencies in British education. I hope it will become clear, in a reading of the chapter, why I have placed such importance on improvement in the general level of education and upon education for all until 18-plus. The techniques and practices of Japanese companies require a breadth and degree of mathematical, communicative, scientific and technological competences that are high in comparison with those attained by the generality of British school leavers whether these be 16-plus or 18-plus products of the system.

What I have chosen to do, therefore, is to work from a point of view that I believe to be both an economic imperative and an economic inevitability. That is, Britain will have to compete with Japan in manufactures and will ultimately, therefore, have to accept the techniques that have made Japan so successful. We shall need to embrace 'Japanization' in just the same way as is currently being done, much to our competitive disadvantage, in the newly industrializing countries of the Asian Pacific Rim (Hofheinz and Calder 1982).

I therefore propose to discuss some of these techniques in the hope that 'what manufacturing industry needs to do' will become clearer. At the same time I hope that the implications for education and training will become obvious.

Even within this limited objective I intend to impose a further restriction. The 'sociology' of Japanese companies is radically different from that in British ones. Indeed, much of the literature on the Japanese economic miracle has concentrated on this and is voluminous. The interested reader is referred to the special bibliography.

There is a problem about 'transferability', inherent in a concentration on the sociological aspects of Japanese companies. I have therefore largely restricted my discussion to physical industrial techniques in which this problem is less contentious and in which, I hope, the economic objectives of education and training will be clearer. The remainder of this chapter will attempt to indicate the desirable outcomes in manufacturing industry of all involved from the boardroom to the shop floor.

SOME BACKGROUND TO BRITISH AND JAPANESE MANUFACTURING

Japan recovered much more quickly from the oil shocks of the 1970s than did the Western economies. Indeed, because Japan is so vulnerable to oil price movements, the recovery was hardly believable in the West. Charges of 'dumping' were common. These can largely be shown as false (Allen 1978). The truth was that Japan had made great advances in manufacturing techniques with the concomitant ability to charge very competitive prices.

The West attempted to cope with its difficulties by political and financial means. Britain seemed to be singularly indirect in confronting the challenge posed by world recession. British government, particularly the Treasury, seemed to be working on the principle of:

concentrating first and foremost on symbolic figures and quantities, like prices, exchange rates and balances of payment, to the neglect of real quantities, like goods and services produced and traded. In particular, the subordination of one to the other is such that whenever there is a clash of interests, the real must be sacrificed to the symbolic.

(Pollard 1981)

There was little attempt to get out of our difficulties by a revamping of industrial performance; it required a decade or more, after the first oil shock, before the urgent need to improve training became nationally accepted.

Japan attacked the problem much more directly by rapid strides in the development of new manufacturing techniques. It is, perhaps, from the principle of 'direct attack' that we have most to learn. An example from the area of management training will illustrate the point.

In April 1987 Professor Charles Handy of the London Business school, reported on the lamentable state of managerial qualification that still exists. Seventy-six per cent of managers, currently operating in Britain, left school at the minimum age with, at most, O-levels or CSEs. Twenty per cent of managers confessed to having no qualifications at all. Only 12.5 per cent had a degree of any sort. Handy's report confirmed the findings of the official Labour Force Survey of 1981 which showed similar results – another six wasted years in which the problem was not tackled! (*Guardian* 29.4.87).

At the same time as the Handy Report, another, by Dr John Constable and Mr Roger McCormick, was prepared for the National Economic Development Council. The NECD report said that the average British manager gets only one day's training a year; 36 per cent of middle managers have had no management training since starting work. Both reports call for a great expansion in management education. The NECD report suggested the introduction of a Diploma in Business Administration with a target output of 35,000 graduates each year. Both reports called for an expansion in MBA-type output with a target of 10,000 graduates per year by the turn of the century (ibid.).

British industry, on average, spends only one and a half pence per £10 of turnover on management training. The USA spends six times this amount and Germany twelve times. The education system, universities, polytechnics, and business schools produce

169

annually only about 12,000 new managers. Industry's needs are for 90,000. The shortfall is made up by people with no management skills at entry to industry (BBC Television).

A comparison with management training and priorities in Japan might reveal that, although Handy, Constable and McCormick have correctly identified problems their solutions may be misdirected. There is a growing body of opinion that believes Britain went wrong when, belatedly, we copied the American type of business school. Professor Cyril Levicki of Queen Mary College, himself a former entrepreneur, thinks that our business schools have become too academic, that they concentrate too much on set formulae which reduce flair and the capacity to take risks. They do not promote willingness to search for new products (BBC Television).

Professor Levicki also worries that some of our business schools do not concentrate enough on applied management education and that many of the tutors have insufficient experience in industry itself – that they make their teaching into 'another faculty-type job'. There may be an over-concentration on board-room problems rather than those of the shop floor.

> Japanese managers have rejected our complex management prescriptions . . . The Japanese way is to simplify. The simple but ingenious production management and quality control approaches . . . seem to travel easily to other Japanese firms without really being taught in . . . business schools or promoted by consultants.
>
> (Schonberger 1982)

This view is supported by Dore and Sako who make the point that:

> Japanese firms rely relatively less on courses provided by training firms or outside consultants, more on mutual teaching, off-the-job as well as on but more often the latter, within the firm.
>
> (Dore and Sako 1989)

Like Britain, Japan had no business school tradition. Japan has found a different route out of this problem. Management training is almost entirely the preserve of private industry capitalizing on the high educational standard of its managerial recruits.

Japan has, however, been as ready to import good management techniques as she has been to import technology. Quality control and quality circles were brought to Japan by two Americans, W.E. Deming and Joseph Juran. To this day the 'Deming Award' is a distinction to which Japanese companies aspire. The Americans did not really take Deming very seriously but he was an instant success in Japan. Juran's *Quality Control Handbook* sold the ideas about quality-management to Japanese business-men who realized that a prime tool had fallen into their hands – that the management ethic could be informed by the search for quality above all else.

The Japanese manufacturing ethos was shaped by the oppor-tunities and problems presented by a very competitive and rapidly expanding home market during the early decades after the war. There has been a high emphasis placed on capture of market share. The most direct ways in which this has been achieved have been through the twin-pronged objectives of quality and competitive price. Both of these depend upon improved production techniques.

MARKET-SHARE PHILOSOPHY

In a market that doubles in size each year – a phenomenon by no means rare in the case of new products or those using new tech-nologies, such as calculators, video recorders and so on – a company must double its output and sales each year simply to retain its share of the market. If the market continues to double each year for 5 years the company will have to increase output and sales by 32 times simply to retain its original share. In Japan's post-war economic boom many companies have had to contend with this and similar magnitudes of growth. Of course a company could elect not to maintain its share of the increasing market, keep its volume of sales constant at the initial level and be satisfied with what it had. However, the situation does not truly offer this as a realistic alternative.

It is a commonplace of the manufacturing process that large-scale production leads to economies in unit costs and/or increas-ing technological refinement. Typically, about a 20 per cent cost reduction can be achieved for each doubling of production. Imagine two companies, A and B, who share equally a market of an initial 1,000 units in which there is an opportunity to double in size each year. Company A decides to take this opportunity but B elects to wait for 3 years to see how things develop, relinquishing all the growth in the market to A. After 3 years of explosive growth, A is 15 times as large a company, in terms of production as B and has over 90 per cent of the market (B has in theory retained its original 500 units of sales; A's sales have risen to 7,500 units). A's prices will be a fraction of B's and probably A will have been able to add new lines to its product range. B, in practice, simply goes out of business. As growth in the market flattens out, A will probably begin to look overseas for export opportunities. It is company A and those like it – the winners in the Japanese home competition – that Western industries have to confront. We seldom encounter B and the other losers; the ones we come up against are Matsushita (Panasonic), Sony, Hitachi, Toshiba and NEC. Walk down your High Street and look at the effect these have had on the production of British consumer electronics.

Medical imaging equipment, with high technological specification, was introduced into Japan in the early 1960s. This was state-of-the-art equipment, supplied at very high prices and was sold in Japan by Western companies with an initial technological lead over the Japanese of about 6 years – ample time, if they had utilized it correctly, to establish an unassailable market share. During this period, Japanese firms began to enter the market with lower-priced, simpler machines which they sold to small clinics and hospitals that were unable to afford the expensive and technically more sophisticated Western products. The latter continued to hold, for a time, the limited market of the large hospitals and research institutions, markets that soon were filled causing a decline in sales growth from an initial high of 20 per cent per annum to only 5 per cent. The Japanese end of the market sustained, from 1976 to 1980, a growth rate of over 80 per cent. High growth and large market share generated a 'winners' cycle' causing the prices of Japanese equipment to come down quickly, enabling, as with the sale of calculators, for instance, more and more customers to enter the market and sustain the growth. In the process, Japanese manufacturers were able to increase the technical performance of their machines to match, and eventually supersede that of the Western imports, whilst pricing them 40 per cent lower. The most advanced machines, those using nuclear magnetic resonance, were introduced by Toshiba and Hitachi a year ahead of their Western rivals (Abegglen and Stalk 1985).

172

SOME JAPANESE MANUFACTURING TECHNIQUES

The just-in-time (JIT) system

Research has shown that up to 70 per cent of the space in a factory may be taken up by storage areas for incoming parts, parts waiting to move on to another stage of manufacturing, holding room for finished products and walkways for moving parts around the factory and in and out of storage. These accumulations have costs – inventory costs – which are surprisingly high. In addition, handling and moving material and parts can be much more expensive than may be apparent. In one study, the management of a factory thought its handling costs were minimal because only 40 out of its 1,000 workers were designated as material handlers. Investigations of the work done by men actually engaged in manufacturing processes, revealed that they were spending a considerable amount of time in handling as well. In fact, in total, handling costs were equivalent to about 300 workers (Abegglen and Stalk 1985).

JIT attempts to resolve two conflicting sets of costs shown in Figure 8.1(a). When the factory changes over its tooling, to switch from the production of one variant in its product line to another, costs are involved in re-tooling and the time machines and men are idle. To make up for this, a long run of the new variant is needed to reduce the unit cost. The re-tooling costs are spread over a large number of units of production. However, as the production run continues, inventory charges increase because the factory is producing parts faster than it can use them in the next stage, or finished products faster than they can be sold. They are, in other words, accumulating stocks to meet demand when that particular production run ends, either for their own needs, in the case of partly finished goods, or for customers for the finished product. At some point, the inventory costs become so great, or storage space becomes so full, that the production run has to be ended and a switch made to another variant. Whilst this next run is taking place stocks held from the previous one will be used up. The total cost (upper curve in Figure 8.1(a)) bottoms out above the intersection of the unit cost curve and the inventory cost curve. The point that this represents on the lower axis is called the economic order quantity or EOQ.

In theory, if the switchover time from one variant to another could be made instantaneously, no switchover costs would be involved. In this case the inventory of any part, or finished product, could be reduced to one. A production run of one unit would be the most economical – any more than one would increase, however slightly, the inventory costs (Figure 8.1(b)). This was the idea that Toyota began to work on.

Figure 8.1 Relationship between production run length, inventory costs, and economic order quantity (EOQ)

(a) Slow switchover (British) manufacturing

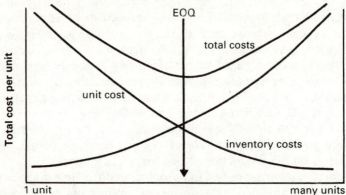

(b) Rapid switchover (Japanese) manufacturing

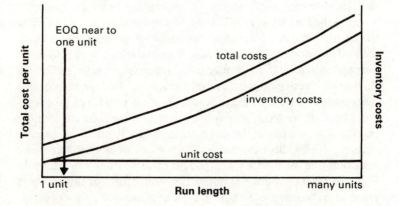

Source: Adapted from Abegglen and Stalk (1985) and Schonberger (1982)

In practice, of course, no machine can be re-tooled so that switchover takes zero time – but reorganization of the factory and the working methods could reduce the time taken to a minimum.

Rapid switchover is achieved by a number of devices. Perhaps the most critical is multi-machine manning. Firms using JIT capitalize on the high degree of education and trainability of their workforce to emphasize worker utilization over machine utilization. The high depreciation allowances against tax make it profitable for Japanese companies to invest in enough machinery to do this. In older forms of manufacturing, the worker acts like a well-behaved French waiter serving the needs of his machine. In multi-machine manning the worker 'uses' a number of machines, in sequence, to perform a manufacturing task. When a machine has completed its work it pauses until the operator returns to it. Movement of parts from one machine to the next is facilitated by handling devices and the layout of the worker's production area. He may, for instance, walk a square, circular or triangular layout of machines depending on the demands of the process he is involved in. The worker will have been trained in routine maintenance of his machines. A multi-machine layout is designed so that each machine can cope with many different variants of the same type of part. It is essential that machines can be re-tooled quickly. Frequently, special re-tooling devices are employed that enable the operator to do this himself. Some variants may need additional machines, these stand idle but set up ready, in the worker's layout, when those particular variants are not being made.

Typically, Japanese engineers expect a 30 to 50 per cent improvement in workers' productivity by the use of multi-machine manning. Yanmar, a maker of diesel engines, increased productivity by 200 per cent in the machining of a wide range of different crankshafts. Mazda made improvements of between 49 per cent and 175 per cent in different parts of its factory. At Yanmar, switchover is so efficient that the factory makes one unit, of every variant it produces, *every 20 minutes* (Abegglen and Stalk 1985). Many Japanese firms use self-developed tools. The managing director of one Japanese electronic consumer goods firm in South Wales explained to me that the factory's increase in both quality and output had been due to the 'invention' on site of a special multi-soldering device by the chief production engineer. Japanese companies also seem much more ready than those in the West to alter machines bought in from specialist suppliers (Schonberger 1982). Adaptations on site have greatly improved Japanese set-up times and re-tooling. The comparatively low representation of engineers in the upper management of British companies may blind us to the economies of improved set-up. The 'accountancy' ethos of upper management is more likely to be concerned with the things it can readily understand from the balance sheet like labour costs, interest on loans and the current share price of the company (Schonberger 1982; Abegglen and Stalk 1985; Kono 1984).

Toyota decided that the speed of the final assembly line should decide the speed at which all the sub-assembly operations should run. This is called the 'pull system'. To take a simple example, the rate at which the final assembly uses a part from a sub-assembly line will determine the speed at which the sub-assembly line is to run – the final assembly 'pulls' the parts through the sub-assembly operation. A stock of the part therefore does not accumulate beyond that quantity needed for immediate production. The part is produced just-in-time to meet the demand. When the final line begins to use its stock of the part it sends back a '*kanban*', or order card, for the next batch to the sub-assembly line for the same number of the part. If the production times have been carefully adjusted, this new order will have been filled just as the final line runs out of its previous stock. The 'pull' system works all the way back through the production process and finally draws in materials from the sub-contractors who deliver, JIT, just the EOQ of the components they supply to the main assembler. The sub-contractor may thus make several small deliveries each day rather than a large supply to cover a long period which would attract inventory costs.

In the theory of JIT, the raw material arrives JIT to be fabricated into components; components JIT to be made into sub-assembly parts; sub-assembly parts JIT to be made into the finished product; and the finished product made JIT to be sold. Nothing stands idle.

If this sounds far-fetched, Nissan has gone one stage better. It has linked 500 suppliers of parts and dealers by a computer network. A customer, in consultation with the dealer, decides he wants a particular car, in a certain colour with a specific interior trim chosen from the company's wide range. This information is fed immediately into a computer by the dealer. This informs the body production line that our customer wants, let us say, a red car with grey seats and other option choices. As the car body enters the spraying line the seat manufacturer receives instructions. Two hours later, just in time, as the car assembly is reaching the appropriate stage of assembly, the seats arrive from the supplier and are fitted immediately. The car is fitted with a computer bar code that specifies the customer requirements. The highly robotized plant reads these as the car passes through assembly and installs the customer's choices automatically. A few minutes later the car is complete and on its way to the dealer's showroom just as it was ordered half a morning previously. This device has enabled Nissan to level its schedule down to the time taken to produce one car, at least as far as the home market served by the computer dealership is concerned.

To regard JIT simply as an inventory reduction and control device, is to miss some of the other major benefits that it confers. Figure 8.2 attempts to summarize these.

A worker in a conventional Western production line produces parts that go into a stockpile. The next operation draws them from this stockpile. Many thousands of parts may be produced before a particular stockpile is used. Some will be defective and the company usually sets an 'acceptable level' of rejects. In JIT as soon as a part is made it is used at the next station down the line. If it is defective this is noticed instantly. Each worker comes to regard the prior operator *personally* as his source of parts. Each worker feels an obligation to the next person down the line to avoid hold-ups. Information about the production of defects is soon highlighted. Thus the JIT system operating through boxes A and B in Figure 8.2 result in scrap control and quality control in box C and information through box F to box E. Workers, production managers, and production engineers, on the shop floor, generate ideas about how things can be improved relative to boxes A, B, and C. Thus, continuous cycles of improvement occur both in production and quality (box D). JIT is not, therefore just a once and for all improvement system.

Many Japanese managements have made deliberate cuts at box F. With less 'buffer', in terms of spare workers and stocks, working practices are sharpened up to avoid defect production. If smooth production can be obtained with reduced buffer this prompts management to make further reductions (arrow from D to F). The beneficial effects of JIT finally accumulate in box L via boxes I, J, F, and K.

The education and training implications of using such a system

Figure 8.2 Benefits of JIT

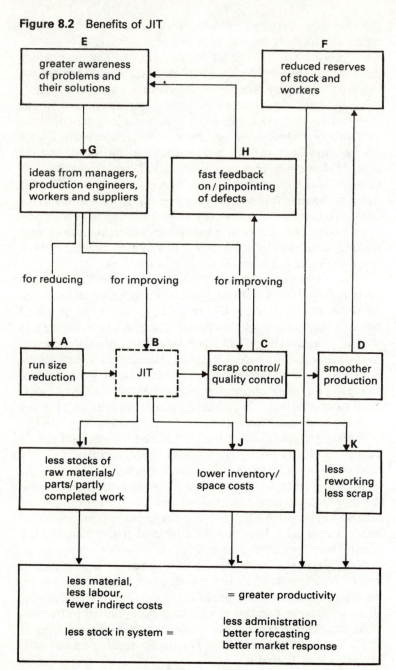

Source: Adapted from Schonberger (1982)

are immense. The cycle of improvement involves workers getting together to define problems and propose solutions. The imperatives and motivations, inherent in tackling highly visible problems may be as much a contributor to the ready formation of quality circles as the 'groupishness' of Japanese culture. JIT may be one of the sources of 'intimacy' in Japanese companies that is a key component of 'Theory Z' (Ouchi 1981). Whether this is true or not, the effectiveness of quality circles is greatly enhanced by the relatively high standard of education amongst the workers. On the training side, an untrained, or poorly trained operative would be an immediate hindrance to his workmates. His shortcomings cannot be hidden in the inventory pile. The multi-skilling of Japanese workers greatly enhances worker flexibility within the JIT system which admits of no protective demarcation rules.

Total quality control

Japanese companies have capitalized upon the quality-enhancing characteristics of JIT to introduce total quality control, TQC. Thus each worker becomes responsible for the quality of his output. Quality control departments, quality inspectors, and so on have been dispensed with. JIT reveals lack of quality at source.

> Everything you hear about the Japanese attitude to quality is true. Commitment to a zero defect product is absolute – not only at top management levels but throughout the company – particularly at the 'sharp end' where the products are actually made. Assembly workers genuinely take a pride in building the perfect product, and insist that the components they receive are of the same high standard.
>
> (Wickens 1987)

The *ability* to produce with quality, however, cannot be ascribed to JIT. JIT simply highlights failure quickly. The ability to produce with quality is a function first of caring and understanding, (educational assets), and of developed skills and capacities (training capitalizing on education). Much of the effectiveness of JIT and TQC can be ascribed to Japan's army of production engineers who monitor, improve, and innovate constantly at shop-floor level. Britain has a dearth of such engineers and those we have are largely undervalued and relatively under-used. The shortage arises directly out of our failure to educate a larger proportion of the population beyond the low horizon of 16-plus. The ability of ordinary Japanese shop-floor workers to contribute to QC discussion reflects the high degree of general education.

However, concepts like QC and zero-defect, nowhere near represent the reality of Japanese total quality control which is a 'whole-organization educational idea' operationalized. It has to be understood by everyone; quality has to be the first priority; the enterprise has to develop the habit of improvement. 'The burden of quality proof . . . rests with the makers of the part' (Feigenbaum 1961) has been re-translated by the Japanese as *'the responsibility for quality'*, a much more proactive view of what is needed to produce with TQC.

Integration of suppliers

The benefits of JIT will be enhanced if the suppliers and sub-contractors have been brought into the system. Most Japanese users of JIT have been at some pains to do this. Perhaps a year ahead of production, a schedule of requirements will be given to the supplier. This may be refined six months later in the light of more sophisticated knowledge of the likely demand. In this revised estimate will be a condition that, at the next revision, figures will not be altered by more than say 20 per cent. The same principle applies at each subsequent revision but the proportion by which the schedule may be altered is reduced at each stage. After some agreed deadline, perhaps a month before production begins, the schedule is frozen and cannot be altered. This gives the supplier a fixed order that he must fulfil. Ideally, parts and materials from sub-contractors and suppliers would be delivered in consignments of a size to match exactly the JIT 'pull through' demand of the final assembly line. More than this quantity will involve the accumulation of unnecessary inventory and handling and their costs; less than the specified delivery and the line will run short of parts and stop – also a costly business. At Toyota these deliveries from the suppliers take place every two hours. It has been found more cost-effective to pay for frequent small deliveries than to pay inventory costs at both the supplier's and Toyota's end of the transaction.

This system, of course, demands very close liaison with suppliers. A metal parts supplier in the North East of England said recently, on a television programme about Komatsu, a company that has just set up in the region, that he sees the buyer from a British factory perhaps once or twice a year. He was seeing the Komatsu buyer sometimes two or three times a day. The competitive strategies of Komatsu's Japanese factories illustrate the advantages of JIT. In the industry that makes heavy construction equipment there is savage competition between Komatsu and the (presently) larger American company Caterpillar. JIT offers two competitive advantages – the same variety of products at lower costs or a wider variety of products at the same cost. Sometimes both advantages accrue simultaneously. From 1980 to 1985 the volume of Komatsu's business grew by 40 per cent whilst that of Caterpillar decreased by 50 per cent. Komatsu currently offers a wider product line than Caterpillar at lower prices. An irony of the story, from Britain's point of view, is that the new Komatsu factory in the North East was previously a Caterpillar factory. The American giant was forced to close down its UK operation under the competition from Komatsu. The high degree of Japanese competitive strength is able to offer employment that the less robust, but larger American firm was unable to sustain.

Vertical integration, to a degree, uses internal transactions to replace market forces that would otherwise affect, individually and separately, the suppliers of materials, the manufacturer, and the sales distribution system. The elements become integrated with one another. Thus a firm like Toyota integrates its 'downstream' suppliers and its 'upstream' dealerships into a coherent system to provide cars for the market. This is not specifically a Japanese business phenomenon. What makes the Japanese form of integration effective is the selectivity over what is integrated. Many Western companies show a degree of integration but have often been less careful than the Japanese about which elements they integrate. They have, for instance, integrated some unimportant processes but have left others out of the integration system (Kono 1984).

An important concept in Japanese integration is that of 'key-process', the holder of which can exert power over the rest of the system and is normally the one that initiates the integration. Thus a car manufacturer is likely to integrate a supplier of gearbox systems but the reverse is unlikely. The manufacturer

181

controls the key process. Production of gearboxes is, however, an important stage in the manufacturing process, it could indeed be considered the next-to-key-process and will therefore be an early target for integration of some kind. It is clearly more important for the manufacturer to integrate the gearbox firm than, for instance, a firm that makes rear-view mirrors. Japanese literature on theories of business define many types and degrees of integration. Two only will suffice here.

In consolidated integration the company would itself undertake the next-to-key-processes or would have a majority holding, and therefore effectively own a subsidiary company that carried out this process. More frequently, in Japan, quasi-vertical integration is found in which the company sub-contracts its next-to-key-processes and does not have a majority holding of the company doing the work (Kono 1984). The dominant company, however, may have exclusivity on the product of the smaller one or at least buy a majority of its output. It is on quasi-vertical integration that I shall concentrate since this is more typically Japanese than other forms but the Seiko case is worth consideration, later, in respect of consolidated integration.

Generally, in quasi-vertical integration, control by the major company is exerted in many ways but these also confer some advantages on the smaller one. To begin with, the relationship is an enduring one that supersedes the legalities of the long-term contracts that are entered into. The large company does not shed the smaller one simply because it finds the possibility of a cheaper source of components. This ensures the source of supply for the large company and an assured continuance for the smaller. Often the key-process company makes loans to the smaller, in order to promote a technological similarity between the two. This ensures a match in the rate of production and quality. Similar effects are achieved by management training given to the smaller company. Processes like JIT depend heavily on a correspondence between technology and managerial expertise in all the firms contributing to the final product. This sort of exchange makes the transfer of technology very rapid in Japan and, in part, accounts for the quick response companies can make to changing technological opportunities.

The Seiko watch company, with a considerable degree of integration of its operation, was able to enter the quartz crystal watch market ahead of and with much greater penetration than the Swiss manufacturers. The Swiss industry, in 1960, had about 500 makers of finished watches and over 1,000 makers of watch components. Seiko produced most of its parts in its own companies and in addition produced the machines to make the parts. It has consolidated the integration of key and next-to-key processes within the firm. The new technology was slow to penetrate the Swiss industry; small component makers were reluctant to change or unable to invest in new technology. Seiko raced ahead in the large-scale production of integrated circuits, liquid crystal, tuning forks, and step-motors (Kono 1984).

Toyota is a company showing a very high degree of quasi-vertical integration. The key-processes are the assembly of the motor vehicle from its myriad parts, the production of the engines, body pressing, and design of the products. These are under the direct control of Toyota and are carried out in its own factories. Next-to-key processes, like making transmission systems, are performed outside the company by suppliers with whom Toyota has formed strong links. Toyota is able to exert a large measure of control over these companies through its dominant position in the transactions that take place between them. Frequently Toyota has at least two suppliers of each of the major components it needs. This reduces its dependencies on just one supplier and weakens the bargaining position of each supplier. About 230 suppliers form the 'Toyota co-operation group' – the *kyohokai*.

On the 'up-stream' side of its operation Toyota has a very powerful sales system with 250 retailers who between them have about 2,900 sales outlets and 33,000 salesmen in Japan alone. The retailers are independent businesses but are controlled by Toyota through long-term contracts and are committed to selling Toyota products only. In the UK, dealers have a much greater measure of independence. Toyota increases the dependence of its sales channel by the provision of benefits to the dealers. It makes loans of various kinds, provides management training and gives advice on planning.

Certain advantages accrue from Japanese-style integration. The technical innovation, for which Japanese companies are famous, is facilitated by the linkages that are formed. Second, it is easier to control and improve quality by an integrated network than in a system of looser linkages. If the sales channel is integrated, a more accurate assessment of demand can be made by the manufacturer. Better service to the customer can be guaranteed as we saw in the case of Nissan's 'made to order cars'. Systems like JIT are greatly enhanced in integrated companies.

POSSIBLE IMPLICATIONS IN BRITAIN

There is much evidence to show that the Japanization of British industry has already begun. Clearly, the leaders in the field are the Japanese companies themselves whose successful operation in this country will set a standard. Many of the industrial giants, Matsushita, Sony, Hitachi, Komatsu, Nissan are already in operation. Some firms like Honda have formed joint ventures with British companies. In spring 1989 negotiations for a new Toyota plant at Derby were completed. In the City the Japanese banks and investment houses are well established.

To date much of the operation of the manufacturing companies has been assembly only. EEC 'anti-screwdriving' legislation will produce a trend towards the incorporation of EEC-produced components into finished products. This need will be fulfilled from two sources: indigenous European companies and smaller Japanese component manufacturers who find it economic to set up here. The way the share in the market becomes allocated will undoubtedly depend on the competitive response of British supplier companies. The Japanese supplier industries will not be slow to take advantage of the opportunity. Already in South Wales, that has Europe's largest concentration of Japanese companies, Electronic Harnesses (UK), a Japanese company making components for the consumer electronics industry, has opened a factory to supply one of the large local assembly plants.

Philip Cousins, managing director of AP Automotive Products, a major components producer makes the point about the need to compete and integrate:

We are moving towards a partnership approach. Those suppliers who do interface directly with manufacturers will have to be world class in reliability and quality, technical competence and innovativeness. They will need large investment in advanced manufacturing techniques, adopt just in time supply philosophy and be world class in competitive terms.

(*Business Wales* May 1989)

If British suppliers are unable to respond – that is to a degree Japanize their operations – the present 'window' of opportunity will be lost. The possible ways in which Japanese companies will exploit this 'window' has been studied in relation to the Nissan plant at Washington in the North East. An excellent reflection on the methods of Nissan is to be found in Wickens (1987). On the particular general issue of Japanization, in another study, six essential features have been listed (Crowther and Garrahan 1987). My comments on these differ to a degree in interpretation, from those of the authors, which have an undertone of disapproval, but agree that the essence of Japanization has been properly identified: (Crowther and Garrahan in inverted commas).

'Relations with the central and local state': The British government has been eager to attract Japanese industry and local government, especially in areas of employment deprivation and has seen Japanese investment as an alleviation of local poverty.

'The approach to organised labour': Through the stipulation of single-union deals Nissan has sought the nearest (presently?) acceptable British equivalent to the Japanese single enterprise union.

'Influence over the industrial environment': Nissan has purchased a site of 733 acres consisting of a core-site where its own factory is located and a further 436 acres over which, subject to local planning regulations, it owns rights of disposal. I agree with Crowther and Garrahan's proposition that the extra land will be used by Nissan to bring its own suppliers into close juxtaposition with the main assembly plant. Whether these are British or Japanese will depend on our competitive abilities and willingness to adapt.

'Determining the supply of components': Suppliers gain the advantage of long-term contracts by entering part mergers – quasi-vertical integration – with Nissan as the dominant partner. For Nissan this is essential to its JIT production process. The power position of Nissan in the arrangement will undoubtedly lead to the incorporation of Japanese manufacturing techniques into the component suppliers' operations.

It will be easier for Nissan to do this, and hence more likely that they choose British suppliers, if the education, training and hence responsiveness of British companies can come to match those of Japanese contenders for the favoured position.

'The JIT system of manufacturing': Nissan was in the favourable position of being able to recruit the pick of the workforce in an area where jobs were at a premium. Nissan's capacity to introduce JIT using a British workforce should therefore not be taken to be generally indicative of our capacity to introduce JIT in less select circumstances. Furthermore, along with JIT a great number of other Japanese company practices were incorporated that depended heavily on the skills and training of a very high-class cadre of managerial and supervisory recruits (Wickens 1987).

'The management of human resources': Nissan is causing a re-think in attitudes to manufacturing. The single-union deal has been reproduced elsewhere, not always without opposition and controversy. It is however, at least, a 'thinkable' development for the future. It would not have been so a decade ago.

Some commentators see in Japanization a real threat to British industry. They fear that it will spell the demise of our indigenous industries, and, if 'screwdriver' plants remain the order of the day, lead to the de-skilling of our workers. One writer sees current Japanization as an industrial 'Trojan Horse' (James 1989). There is reason behind these fears. My own view is that we shall have to compete with the Japanese whether we have their companies in our own country or not. Having them here might be a more effective and perceivable stimulus to a shake-out in industry, education, and training.

SOME TRAINING IMPLICATIONS

Clearly, things have to change in British training. Not least, attitudes have to undergo some sharp revision from top to bottom. Gavin Laird of the engineers' union summed up the situation in the following way:

[It is] difficult to single out one particular problem with British industry but if challenged to do that, the lack of resources in training and education seems to me the largest and most difficult problem we are facing.

(Television)

The British workforce is sometimes resistant to responsibility and promotion. A Japanese manager, of a company operating in Britain, expressed some surprise to me on this point. He was greatly mystified, having offered training and the prospect of promotion to several workers to have his offer declined. The men preferred to remain at a lower level of status and pay. For a time he was only half convinced by my assurances that he had not made some mistake in his approach. He believed that he had blundered into some cultural problem and had provoked the refusal by his own ineptitude. On the next attempt he delegated the approach to a British manager. The result was the same. Other Japanese companies, my friend tells me, have since encountered an identical problem. They are utterly dumbfounded by it. On the brighter side, the younger generation of employees show more willingness to stretch their wings than the over-35 age group where attitudes to industry have become entrenched. Ironically it is the 35- to 40-year-old cohort, who have mastered the techniques of the shop floor, and have developed in wisdom and maturity, who are ripe for promotion. One very famous Japanese company in Wales tried to get rid of its over 35s so that it could start with a clean slate of younger and more adaptable workers.

There is one factor of the international economy that makes training vital to our survival. Newly industrializing countries are able to compete with our traditional industries on very favourable labour-cost terms. Unless we, with our relatively higher labour costs, can produce efficiency through technology we have little chance of competing on the world scene in price terms. Better still we should train our workforce towards the highest technology and leave the traditional industries to the emergent economies.

Britain could, conceivably, experience a short-term fall in unemployment by growth in output of the same products by the same techniques. This would not, however, solve the underlying problem. Indeed, the trade figures for late 1988 and early 1989 show an alarming increase in balance of payments deficits. This is in no small measure the result of increased spending on imported consumer goods that our manufacturing base cannot produce or cannot produce at competitive prices or with the right quality.

If our low-tech industries were allowed to continue in the same old way, the temporary improvement in employment statistics would soon reverse, once more, into decline. This would result from yet another, and inevitable, wave of new technology that would leave them even further behind than they are now. Already, according to a recent survey by Davies and Caves for the National Institute for Social and Economic Research our eight best performing industries were 40 per cent below the productivity of those in America. Our eight worst performing industries fell 75 per cent below those of America (*Guardian* 29.5.87).

On a per capita basis Japan graduates each year four times as many engineers as Britain, three times as many as the USA and 70 per cent more than West Germany. In gross numbers, in the 1980s, Japan has been turning out 75,000 engineers each year compared with Britain's 9,000. In Britain there has been a huge disparity between the numbers of engineering graduates and those in the theoretical physical sciences. This may explain why Britain has accomplished so many scientific breakthroughs without, subsequently, being able to capitalize on them. Modern industrial success depends more on engineers and technologies than it does on pure scientists, or at least, the number of engineers acts as a limiting factor given an adequate number of scientists. Britain's industrial progress, at present, is clearly rate-limited by a shortage of engineers.

The MSC/NEDC skills monitoring reports reveal the acute shortage of engineers: 'In the engineering industry the outlook is appalling. The number of workers undergoing training in that sector halved between 1978 and 1984' (*Observer* 22.2.87).

And in a report to the Commons, the Engineering Industry Training Board argued that: 'The industry has never been faced with the need to retrain adults on the scale and with the urgency now required and the issue is largely unrecognized by employers' (ibid.).

Given that Britain can overcome its attitudinal distaste for engineering, can we produce sufficient engineers in the future? The present nature of the education system makes this unlikely. In a nutshell we teach far too little mathematics and science to a sufficiently advanced age. We have a very limited pool in which to fish.

Because of Britain's poor manufacturing performance, industry is in no position to offer to engineers state-of-the-art training in the new technologies. Engineering training has slumped into a vicious circle of low engineering competence leading to a declining manufacturing base. This results in failure to keep up with the new technologies which in turn completes the circle by depriving engineers of the experience and training they need for the future. We shall see that in Japan the opposite applies and a virtuous circle operates.

Specifically in the training of engineers, the area in which Britain is so deficient, Japan is forging ahead at breakneck speed. The Hitachi company, for instance, has five institutions that are exclusively or partially devoted to training engineers. The Hitachi Institute of Technology runs courses for updating the company's engineers and for broadening their education generally. There are two technical colleges that offer 15-month courses to high-school graduates. In Ibaraki prefecture is the Hitachi Comprehensive Management Research Centre which trains personnel for all levels of management. Many of those passing through this institution are, of course, engineers. The promotion of these men through the levels of management ensures that the company continues to place a high value on engineering training. Finally Hitachi runs a centre devoted to education in production engineering. The courses are open to non-engineers as well as to engineers. The activities of the centre ensure that there is a wide appreciation of the problems of production engineering in all management personnel. At the beginning of this decade Hitachi was spending £30 million a year on its training and education facilities, enough to qualify it as a major university. It expects all its engineers to engage themselves in a life-long learning process.

A survey of Japanese engineers in 1977 showed that 50 per cent of the engineers recruited by Nippon Electrical Company (NEC) in the period 1960–65 felt that it had taken about 12 years for their knowledge, at entry to the company, to become out of date in comparison to the company's current operations. However most of the recent entrants to the company thought that their university training was no longer sufficient after only 2 years with the company. The difference in the figures indicates the accelerating rate of change in modern technology, not a decline in the standards of university education. To counter this problem NEC set up its Institute of Technology Education.

Within 4 years the institute had retrained 1,500 company engineers who had voluntarily applied for courses. Engineers do not apply in order to enjoy a sabbatical away from work – one of the conditions for entry to training is that normal work continues. The course instructors, similarly, teach in addition to performing their other functions within the company. Courses involve the engineer in seminars for a half day every two weeks for six months followed by six months in which he writes a technical paper under the supervision of an instructor. Much of the study, therefore, has to be done in the engineer's own time. There are also courses that aim at a post-graduate level and involve the trainee in attendance one day per week for 12 months. The Institute runs a variety of short courses of 10 to 20 days to meet specific requests from company engineers.

The training of engineers, post-graduation, in the major companies is replacing post-graduate study in the universities. Engineers, in the large companies, are guaranteed contact with state-of-the-art technology, studies directly relevant to production and the assurance that learning will be on a lifetime basis. In a very real sense companies have contributed to the ethos of the learning culture.

The training and development of workers that takes place in the co-operative interactions of workers at the work station has been of immense importance to the development of Japanese industry. By now the quality circles that operate within many Japanese companies are well known. In the west generally, they are regarded primarily as one of the devices a Japanese firm employs to ensure the high quality of its product. Less often is it realized that these also promote the function of staff development. Small groups of workers, engaged in some aspect of the manufacturing process, meet together regularly to discuss matters relating to work. The interaction of human beings, who are thinking about their jobs, reveals ways in which the work process could be changed to improve the quality of the product or to ensure greater efficiency. Members of a group may even wish to complain that the process is too demanding and more efficient ways to relieve the burden, may be sought. Group discussion generates a number of subtle psychological effects which enhance the interest the workers take in their jobs, encourage them to think about what they are doing, and help them learn from one another. This type of meeting creates a fertile seed bed for the training process. A worker whose interest has been captured is more likely to welcome training and to benefit from it.

The activities of groups are reinforced by job rotation and multi-skilled work targeting. A recent innovation has been the 'key worker' concept in which a highly skilled worker assumes a leadership role in group discussion and in the work processes of the group. The key worker is likely to have been given instructor training by the company and is thus in a position to help disseminate knowledge to his group. This assists in both formal and informal training and promotes group cohesion. Job rotation ensures that skills, ideas, working practices, and the ethos of training are spread through the company. As a worker moves from one job, and its associated group of workers, to another, he takes with him knowledge gained in his former group for the benefit of his new one.

Many companies, like JVC who make video recorders, are attempting to blur the distinction between blue- and white-collar workers. Equal emphasis is placed on production and administrative training. There is annual evaluation of workers. When the company believe that a worker is ready for promotion into management one of his attributes most highly valued is his ability to teach others. Under this kind of company ethos training is bound to flourish.

The training ethos of Japanese companies supports the 'less formal' acquisitions at the work station and in the small groups. Toshiba's statement of company philosophy has eight items. For the purposes of this chapter the fourth of these is the most important.

> Toshiba provides its staff members (all its permanent workers) with the opportunity to realise their full potential and cultivate their abilities to the utmost.
>
> (Kasuya 1986)

This aim is translated into 10 objectives that the company tries to meet in its manpower development schemes. A summary of these will reveal the philosophy, and practice, of a company like Toshiba. A similar picture emerges from other large corporations.

Toshiba regards on-the-job-training, OJT, as the core of

manpower development, that is, it should occur during the process of the working in the company. Toshiba expects that, through OJT, the worker will master many skills thoroughly. By aiming to perform with competence and responsibility; by initiating action; overcoming difficulties and seeking original ideas every employee can reach his full potential. The second objective concerns worker 'self-enlightenment' (*jiko keihatsu*). If the translation here carries overtones of Zen I must apologize to the reader. Toshiba's view of 'self-enlightenment' is the development of the will to improve himself on the part of the employee. Without this motivation the company recognizes that it can only accomplish limited training. 'Self-motivation' might have been a better rendering of the spirit if not the letter, of this objective. Toshiba regards management as having a big part to play in developing 'self-enlightenment' in members of its workforce. The company also realizes that it has to provide financial support to the employee's development. The third and fourth objectives develop the theme of responsibility, stressing the importance of the immediate superior's role in assisting and guiding the development of any individual and the part that central management, in each of the company's divisions, must play. The fifth aim is to make off-the-job training (Off.JT) as realistic as possible, specific, and tailored to the needs of each individual concerned. Points six and seven relate to the need for organizational structures and personnel departments to be congruent with the training programmes of the company. It is the personnel department's task to compile comprehensive human inventory systems and career development programmes. The eighth point is concerned with specially gifted employees who ought to be developed according to long-term career objectives. During training and job rotation a close watch must be kept for potential executives. Point nine acknowledges the importance of the employee's character for his development potential. The final point stresses that the programmes are for everyone in the company.

Toshiba spends about £13 million a year on training. It has invested in an impressive training centre at Kawasaki for Off.JT that was constructed in 1960. This incorporates a technology school, computer school, advanced technical training school, adult school, and a technical training centre. Orientation courses for new recruits, basic, advanced and special courses are run from this establishment. The company gives extensive support for learning outside the company through industry-university links, academic societies, correspondence courses, and programmes for study abroad. These are aimed principally at managers, aspiring managers, specialists, and for the training of individuals who are thought promotable to foremen. The activities in off-the-job training conform to a medium-term manpower plan. At the same time on-the-job training, the co-operation between small groups of workers, and the continuous pervasiveness of the training ethos at the work station, combine with the knowledge gained from Off.JT to fulfil the company's master plan for manpower development.

Dore and Sako (1989) identify nine common (British) assumptions about vocational training that Japan brings into question. Two of them, that apply just as well to education, will be a fitting ending to this book:

- That the most important thing is to get the most talented people well trained.

Japan's advantage both in education and training seems to lie in the high average standards of its workforce. It does not concentrate its efforts on the most talented. Particularly, in comparison with Britain, the high educational standard of its middle-of-the-range workers is high. Comparison with the bottom half of our ability range is exceptional: 'A system [ours] that concentrates on giving a small elite a very high standard of education post-16, while shamefully neglecting the rest, cannot be in the interests of the country as a whole' (Judith Judd, *Observer* 28.5.89).

- That industry must use its board and council membership to influence the school and higher education system to be more responsive to industry's needs.

Japan's education system is not influenced very much by 'industry's needs' – whatever these might be. Few operational links exist. Japanese industry seems content to receive recruits with a good educational background and breadth of study. Our agonies over what industry wants from education, our attempts to produce curricular links, and our tendency to introduce vocational elements into what ought to be general education have probably been a waste of time.

References

Note: Only a selection of newspaper articles mentioned in the text have been included here.

Abegglen, J.C. and the Boston Consulting Group (1971) *Business Strategies for Japan*, Tokyo: Sophia University with TBS Britannica Co. Ltd.

Abegglen, J.C. and Stalk, G. (1985) *Kaisha: The Japanese Corporation*, New York: Basic Books.

Allen, G.C. (1978) *How Japan Competes: A Verdict on Dumping*, London: Institute of Economic Affairs.

Anderson, A. (1987) 'Adult training: private industry and the Nicholson letter', in Education and Training UK 1987, A. Harrison and J. Gretton, (eds), *Policy Journals*.

Baker, K. (1989) Secretary of State's Speech to the North of England Conference, 6 January.

Bandura, A. (1982) 'Self-efficacy mechanism in human agency', *American Psychologist*, 37.

Barnett, C. (1987) *The Audit of War*, London: Papermac.

Becker, G.S. (1975) *Human Capital*, 2nd edn, New York: Columbia University Press.

Business Wales (1989) 'Wales: the drive for quality', May, no. 7, Cardiff: Western Mail.

Carrington, J.C. and Edwards, G.T. (1981) *Reversing Economic Decline*, London: Macmillan.

Chapman, P. and Tooze, M. (1987) *The Youth Training Scheme in the UK*, Aldershot: Avebury.

Clark, R. (1979) *The Japanese Company*, Newhaven and London: Yale University Press.

Clegg, H. (1972) *The System of Industrial Relations in Great Britain*, Oxford: Basil Blackwell.

Cmnd 9469 (1985) *Better Schools*, London: HMSO.

Coates, D. and Hillard, J. (eds) (1986) *Economic Decline of Modern Britain*, Brighton: Wheatsheaf Books.

Coleman, D.C. (1973) 'Gentlemen and players', *Economic History Review* 2nd series, vol. 26, no. 1.

Comber, L. and Keeves, J. (1973) *Science Achievement in Nineteen Countries*, New York: John Wiley.

Crowther, S. and Garrahan, P. (1987) 'Invitation to Sunderland: corporate power and the local economy' paper presented to the Conference on the Japanization of British Industry, UWIST, Cardiff, 17 and 18 September.

Daley (1987) *The Independent* (cartoon) 15 January.

DES (1985 March) *Science 5–16: a Statement of Policy*, London: HMSO.

DES (1987) *Statistical Bulletin*, 6/87, London: HMSO.

DES (1987 July) *The National Curriculum 5–16: a Consultation Document*, London: HMSO.

DES and WO (1987) *National Curriculum, Task Group on Assessment and Testing – A Report*, December, London: HMSO.

DES (1988 April) *Advancing A Levels*, London: HMSO.

DES and WO (1988 August) National Curriculum Working Group for Mathematics *Mathematics for Ages 5 to 16*, London: HMSO.

DES and WO (1988 August) National Curriculum Working Group for Science *Science for ages 5 to 16*, London: HMSO.

Dore, R.P. (1987) *Taking Japan Seriously*, London: Athlone Press.

Dore, R.P. and Sako, M. (1987) *Vocational Education and Training in Japan*, a study commissioned by MSC, London: MSC.

Dore, R.P. and Sako, M. (1988) 'Teaching or testing: the role of the state in Japan', *Oxford Review of Economic Policy*, vol. 4, no. 3, autumn.

Dore, R.P. and Sako, M. (1989) *How the Japanese Learn to Work*, Nissan Institute/Routledge Japanese Studies Series, London: Routledge.

Drew, M. (1986) 'Mathematics education in Japan', *Japan Education Journal*, 30, London: Japan Information Centre.

Economist 27 May and 3 June 1967, *The Risen Sun*.

Feigenbaum, A.V. (1961) *Total Quality Control: Engineering and Management*, New York: McGraw-Hill.

Finegold, D. and Soskice, D. (1988) 'The failure of training in Britain: analysis and prescription', *Oxford Review of Economic Policy*, vol. 4, no. 3, autumn.

Fonda, N. and Hayes, C. (1988) 'Education, training and business performance', *Oxford Review of Economic Policy*, vol. 4, no. 3, autumn.

Garden, J. (1986) *The Second International Study of Achievement in Mathematics*, unpublished, in Lynn (op. cit.) and *Japan Educational Journal*.

Goldthorpe, J.H. (1980) *Social Mobility and Class Structure*, Oxford: Clarendon Press.

Goldthorpe, J.H. and Payne, C.W. (1986) 'Intergenerational social mobility in England and Wales 1972–83', *Sociology*, 20.

Hall, P. (1986) *Governing the Economy*, Oxford: Polity Press.

Hedberg, H. (1972) *Japan's Revenge*, London: Pitman.

HMI (1988) *Interim Report on GCSE*, March, London: HMSO.

Hofheinz, R. and Calder, K. (1982) *The Eastasia Edge*, New York: Basic Books.

Hoggart, R. (1971) *The Uses of Literacy: Aspects of Working Class Life, With Special Reference to Publications and Entertainments*, London: Chatto & Windus.

Husen, T. (1967) *International Study of Achievement in Mathematics: A Comparison of Twelve Countries*, New York: John Wiley.

Ienaga, S. (1968) *Taiheiyo Senso*, Tokyo: Iwanami.

Jackson, B. and Marsden, D. (1962) *Education and the Working Class*, Harmondsworth: Pelican Books.

Jackson, M. (1988) 'More leavers shun Youth Training Scheme', *Times Educational Supplement*, 19 February.

James, B.G. (1989) *Trojan Horse: the Ultimate Challenge to Western Industry*, London: Mercury.

Jenkins, R. (1989) *European Diary, 1977–1981*, Collins, extract in *Observer* 12 February 1989.

Khan, H. (1971) *The Emerging Japanese Superstate*, London: Andre Deutsch.

Kasuya, K. (1986) 'Development of human resources for better performance: a Japanese experience' (unpublished paper).

Keep, E. (1986) *Designing the Stable Door: a Study of How the Youth Training Scheme was Planned*, Warwick Papers in Industrial Relations no. 8, May.

Keep, E. and Mayhew, K. (1988) 'The assessment: education, training and economic performance', *Oxford Review of Economic Policy*, vol. 4, no. 3, autumn.

Kogan, M. (1971) *The Politics of Education*, Harmondsworth: Penguin.

Kono, T. (1984) *Strategy and Structure of Japanese Enterprises*, London: Macmillan.

Lewin, K. (1935) *A Dynamic Theory of Personality*, New York: McGraw-Hill.

Locke, E.A., Shaw, K.N., Saari, L.M., and Latham, G.P. (1981) 'Goal setting and task performance: 1969–1980', *Psychological Bulletin*, 90.

Locke, R.R. (1984) *The End of the Practical Man: Entrepreneurship and Higher Education in Germany, France and Great Britain, 1880–1940*, Greenwich, Conn. and London: Jai Press.

Lynn, R. (1988) *Educational Achievement in Japan: Lessons for the West*, London: Macmillan.

Maclure, S. (1988a) *Education Reformed*, Sevenoaks: Hodder & Stoughton.

Maclure, S. (1988b) *Promises and Piecrust*, Southampton: Community Unit TVS.

Macmillan, H. (1975) 'Oxford remembered', *The Times*, 18 October.

Maddison, A. (1987) 'Growth and slowdown in advanced capitalist economies', *Journal of Economic Literature*, 25.

Mayer, C. (1987) 'The assessment: financial systems and corporate investment', *Oxford Review of Economic Policy*, winter.

Miliband, R. (1973) *The State in Capitalist Society*, London: Quartet Books.

Mobley, M., Emerson, C., Goddard, I., Goodwin, S., and Letch, R. (1986) *All About GCSE*, London: Heinemann.

Monbusho (1983) *Monbu Tokei Yoran* (Statistical Abstract of Education Science and Culture): Tokyo.

Morita, A. (1986) *Made in Japan*, London: Collins.

Murphy, J. (1989) 'Graduation Daze', *Times Educational Supplement*, 20 January.

National Council on Education Reform (English translation) (1986 April 23), Tokyo.

National Institute for Educational Research (1983) *Basic Facts and Figures about the Educational System in Japan*, Tokyo.

NEDC (1984) *Competence and Competition: Training in the Federal Republic of Germany, the United States and Japan*, London: NEDD/MSC.

Nelmes, D. (1987) 'Lack of basic skills is a complex problem', *The Listener*, 5 February.

New, C. and Meyers, A. (1986) *Managing Manufacturing Operations in the UK, 1975–1985*, Institute of Manpower Studies.

Obunsha (annually) *Examination Papers for Entrance into Senior High Schools* (in Japanese), Obunsha Publishing House.

OECD (1985) *Education and Training After Basic Schooling*, Paris.

Ouchi, W. (1981) *Theory Z: How American Business Can Meet The Japanese Challenge*, Reading, Mass.: Addison Wesley.

Owen, D. (1986) *A United Kingdom*, Harmondsworth: Penguin.

Passow, H.H., Noah, H.J., Eckstein, M.A., and Mallea, J.R. (1976) *The National Case Study: An Empirical Comparative Study of Twenty One Educational Systems*, Stockholm: Almqvist and Wiksell.

Pollard, S. (1981) *The Wasting of the British Economy*, London: Croom Helm.

Postlethwaite, N. (1988) 'English last in science', *Guardian*, 1 March.

Prais, S.J. (1987) 'Educating for productivity: comparisons of Japanese and English schooling and vocational preparation', *National Institute Economic Review*, February.

Reid, G.L. (1980) 'The research needs of British policy makers' in A. McIntosh, *Employment Policy in the UK and the US*, London: John Martin.

Rohlen, T.P. (1983) *Japan's High Schools*, California: University of California Press.

Sanderson, M. (1972) *The Universities and British Industry 1850–1970*, London: Routledge & Kegan Paul.

Sanderson, M. (1975) *The Universities in the Nineteenth Century*, London: Routledge & Kegan Paul.

Scarborough, H. (1986) 'The politics of technological change at BL', in O. Jacobi *et al.* (eds) *Technological Change, Rationalisation and Industrial Relations*.

Schonberger, R.J. (1982) *Japanese Manufacturing Techniques*, New York: The Free Press.

Secondary Heads Association (1988) *A Levels: The Way Forward*, occasional paper 88/2, November.

Smithers, A. and Robinson, P. (1988) *Securing the future: the shortage of mathematics and physics teachers*, commissioned by Engineering Council, Secondary Heads Association and Headmasters' Conference.

Steedman, H. and Wagner, K. (1987) 'A second look at productivity, machinery and skills in Britain and West Germany', *National Institute Economic Review*, November.

Stigler, J.W., Lee, S., Lucker, G.W., and Stephenson, H.W. (1982) 'Curriculum and achievement in mathematics: a study of elementary

197

school children in Japan, Taiwan and the United States', *Journal of Educational Psychology*, 74.

Stockwin, J.A.A. (1975) *Japan: Divided Politics in a Growth Economy*, London: Weidenfeld & Nicolson.

Streeck, W. (1985) 'Industrial change and industrial relations in the motor industry: an international overview', Lecture at University of Warwick, 23.10.85.

Taylor, C. (1988) 'Climbing towards a skilful revolution', *TES*, 22 January.

Tolman, E.C. (1932) *Purposive Behaviour in Animals and Men*, New York: Appleton-Century-Crofts.

Villiers, Sir C. (1984) *Start Again Britain*, London: Quartet Books.

Vogel, E. (1979) *Japan as Number One: Lessons for America*, New York: Harvard University Press.

Walberg, H.J., Harnisch, D.L., and Tsai, S. (1985) 'Mathematics productivity in Japan and Illinois' (unpublished) in Lynn (op. cit.).

Welsh Office Circular 36/88 *Education Reform Act 1988: Local Management of Schools*, Cardiff: Welsh Office.

White, M. (1988) 'Educational policy and economic goals', *Oxford Review of Economic Policy*, vol. 4, no. 3, autumn.

Whitley, D.J., Wilson, R.A., and Smith, D.J.E. (1980) 'Industrial and occupational change', in R.M. Lindley (ed.) *Economic Change and Employment Policy*, London: Macmillan.

Wickens, P. (1987) *The Road to Nissan: Flexibility, Quality, Teamwork*, London: Macmillan.

Wilensky, H. and Turner, L. (1987) *Democratic Corporatism and Policy Linkages*, Berkeley: Institute of International Studies.

Wolf, M.J. (1983) *The Japanese Conspiracy: Their Plot to Dominate Industry Worldwide and How to Deal with It*, USA: Empire Books.

FOR FURTHER READING ON JAPAN

Economics, industry, and business

Allen, G.C. (1981) *A Short Economic History of Modern Japan*, London: Macmillan.

Allen, G.C. (1981) *The Japanese Economy*, London: MacMillan.

Dore, R.P. (1973) *British Factory–Japanese Factory*, Los Angeles: University of California Press.

Furstenberg, F. (1974) *Why The Japanese Have Been So Successful in Business*, London: Leviathan House.

Guillain, R. (1969) *The Japanese Challenge*, London: Hamish Hamilton.

Hirschmeier, J. and Yui, T. (1975) *The Development of Japanese Business*, London: Allen & Unwin.

Magaziner, I.C. and Hout, T.M. (1980) *Japanese Industrial Policy*, London: Policy Studies Institute.

Nomura Research Institute (1978) *Investing in Japan*, Cambridge: Woodhead-Faulkner.

Okita, S. (1980) *The Developing Economies and Japan*, Tokyo: University of Tokyo Press.

Pascale, R.T. and Athos, A.G. (1981) *The Art of Japanese Management* (with introduction by Sir Peter Parker 1986), Harmondsworth: Penguin.

Roberts, J.G. (1973) *Mitsui: Three Centuries of Japanese Business*, New York and Tokyo: Weatherhill.

White, M. and Trevor, M. (1983) *Under Japanese Management*, London: Policy Studies Institute.

Woronoff, J. (1984) *Japan's Commercial Empire*, London: MacMillan.

Yamamura, K. (1967) *Economic Policy in Post-war Japan*, Los Angeles: University of California Press.

Social history

Austin, L. (ed.) (1976) *Japan: The Paradox of Progress*, New Haven and London: Yale University Press.

Baerwald, H.H. (1974) *Japan's Parliament: an Introduction*, London: Cambridge University Press.

Beasley, W.G. (1963) *The Modern History of Japan*, New York: Praeger.

Christopher, R.C. (1984) *The Japanese Mind*, London: Pan Books.

Dore, R.P. (1976) *The Diploma Disease*, London: George Allen & Unwin.

Kamata, S. (1982) *Japan in the Passing Lane*, London: Counterpoint.

Nakane, C. (1970) *Japanese Society*, London: Pelican.

Japan: An International Comparison (issued yearly free by Japan Information Centre London).

Index

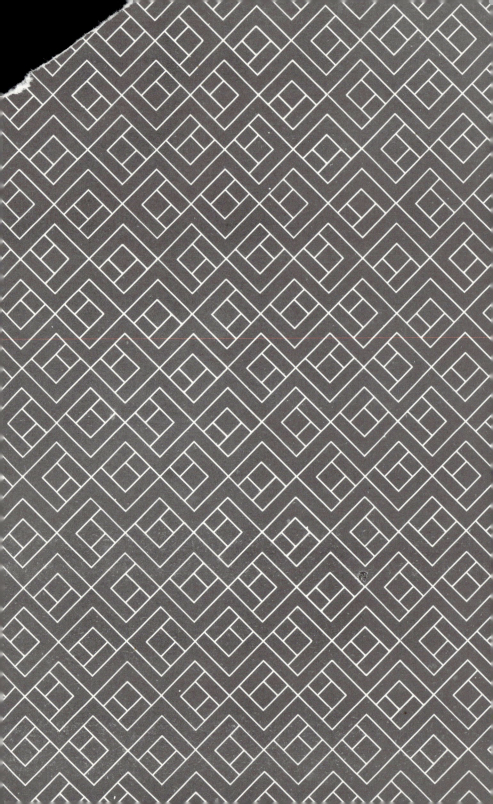